MARCUS AT HOME

MARCUS AT HOME

MARCUS WAREING

Recipe Consultant: Chantelle Nicholson
Recipe Editor: Jo Pratt
Photography: Jonathan Gregson

NOTES ON INGREDIENTS

Unless otherwise stated:

Use large free-range eggs

Use whole milk (but semi-skimmed
can be substituted, if you like)

Use unsalted butter

Use standard plain flour

Use medium-sized fruit and vegetables

Use medium-sized meat and fish portions
(a medium-sized fish portion is 170–180g and
a medium-sized meat portion is 200–220g)

Use fresh herbs – 1 bunch = 25g

HarperCollins*Publishers*
1 London Bridge Street
London SE1 9GF

www.harpercollins.co.uk

First published by HarperCollins*Publishers* 2016

Text © Marcus Wareing 2016
Photography © Jonathan Gregson 2016

10 9 8 7 6 5 4 3 2 1

A catalogue record of this book is available from the
British Library.

ISBN 978-0-00-818447-6

Food styling: Marina Filippelli
Prop styling: Jo Harris

Printed and bound in Spain

MIX
Paper from
responsible sources
FSC C007454

FSC™ is a non-profit international organisation established to promote the
responsible management of the world's forests. Products carrying the FSC
label are independently certified to assure consumers that they come from
forests that are managed to meet the social, economic and ecological needs
of present and future generations, and other controlled sources.

Find out more about HarperCollins and the environment at
www.harpercollins.co.uk/green

CONTENTS

Introduction

I am often asked if I cook at home, and if I do, what I like to cook. To answer the first question, yes, I do cook at home. It is something that I currently enjoy more than ever. Supermarkets, local markets and online shopping have created an amazing 'pantry' for home cookery, and you can now purchase incredible ingredients for your home kitchen that you could only ever source from specialised suppliers when I was growing up. As a young boy, home-cooked food was all we ever ate because my father was a fruit and potato merchant in Southport. He would always bring home a plentiful supply of fruit and vegetables, so it made up a huge part of our diet. His favourite thing was King Edward potatoes, which we ate a lot of! He would always use the older, more ripe produce, too, so nothing was ever wasted.

This was the first part of my education as a cook, unbeknown to me at the time – to use seasonal and ripe ingredients to get the best flavour, and not to waste a thing. There is always a use for overripe fruit and vegetables – jams, chutneys, crumbles, soups and stocks. For me, cooking at home was something I didn't do much when I was in my 20s and 30s, as I was too busy with my career. However, since having children, and since my restaurant group has become more established, I enjoy cooking at home more and more, and I see my home as a great place to enjoy my cooking and being with my family, somewhere I can pass on my passion for food and cookery to my kids.

My ethos as a cook is that it is my job to enhance the natural flavours of ingredients, not to make them look and taste like something else. Mother Nature – along with our farmers and producers – creates the perfect raw ingredients. It is up to us to add the extra touch, something magical that makes you smile when you eat. Sometimes all this takes is a pinch of salt, a squeeze of lemon, a splash of vinegar or a glug of wine – such as when you have a sun-ripened tomato in your back garden in the middle of summer. But sometimes it requires an extra stage or technique in the recipe to really lift the dish.

You will see British ingredients used a lot in my recipes. We have some of the best artisan suppliers here in this country and I use as many of them as I can across my restaurants and at home. In this book I would also like to show you how we find these great ingredients, prepare them, cook them and serve them. I am also a huge fan of ingredients from mainland Europe, which we are very lucky to have on our doorstep. When I was young we went to Spain, Portugal, France and Italy for family holidays, which introduced me to a whole range of foods that I had not experienced before. This, in turn, inspired my cooking later in life. I already had the knowledge of the ingredients and flavours – I just had to learn how to put them together.

When I am asked by our restaurant guests about cooking at home and how to make certain dishes, I always give them the same advice: start with great ingredients. This doesn't mean the most expensive ingredients; it just means produce that is in season, ripe and – where it needs to be – fresh. If you do make recipes with unripe fruit and vegetables you simply won't get a great result. The dish will lack flavour and texture, which no amount of seasoning will change.

Right recipe, right time

This book is divided into four main chapters, which I feel reflects how you most often cook at home. We all lead busy lives and need to organise our weeks more than we ever used to. With this in mind I have grouped the recipes into Midweek, Weekend, Entertaining and Baking. All the recipes are suited to any home environment, and only a few require more specialised equipment, such as an ice cream maker. I have written these recipes for the home cook, but chefs will also find inspiration here for a few interesting flavour combinations. The recipes have been inspired by my own restaurant kitchens and my home cooking.

The Midweek chapter features great family-friendly recipes that are fairly quick to prepare. One of my favourites is the Wareing Family Lasagne on page 41, which is one that my wife Jane has perfected over the years. It is great comfort food and packed full of flavour. For a midweek treat I also really love the Burnt Honey Ice Cream on page 78; it has a really rich and intense flavour, without being too sweet.

The Weekend chapter has recipes that may take a little more time and that can be enjoyed at a more leisurely pace, often with friends or all the family together. The Pulled Pork Sliders with Apple and Ginger on page 118 are always a crowd-pleaser at my house. For a dinner for two, try the Steak with Peppercorn Sauce and Homemade Chips on page 128.

Or the Aromatic Poached and Barbecued Chicken on page 108 is brilliant for a barbecue with friends. The Pumpkin and Maple Custards on page 166 are delicious, as well as being a very interesting new thing to try.

The Entertaining chapter has the most complex recipes, but all of these are achievable at home without a brigade of chefs behind you! They do take the most time to prepare but are worth the extra effort. Plan in advance what you will cook and get as much of the cooking done before the meal so that you too can enjoy it. The Watercress Soup with Soft-Poached Egg and Mustard Crumb on page 174 is a vibrant and peppery soup that can be served hot or cold and can be made in advance. The Braised Oxtail Ravioli on page 202 is also an interesting recipe, as instead of using traditional pasta it uses Asian gyoza wrappers. As a great finale, you must also try the Buttermilk Panna Cotta with Rhubarb and Thyme Crumble on page 229 – it is a lovely, bright, winter dish.

Some of my favourite cakes and easy-to-make breads are included in the Baking chapter, as well as some great recipes to make with children of all ages. The Lemon Yoghurt Cake on page 260 is great for anyone with gluten or dairy intolerances – and it tastes amazing, too. Also try the Chocolate Chunk Cookies on page 267 – delicious warm with a nice cup of tea.

New ways to cook

As a classically trained chef, butter, cream and fats have always been used without much thought to their impact on our bodies. In today's world we are all a lot more conscious of what we put into our bodies and the effect of these ingredients on our health. My approach – as a chef and as a father – is all about knowing what you are eating and then eating the foods that are not hugely healthy in moderation. Food should be enjoyed, and eating, now more than ever, is a great way to catch up with friends and family. So keep learning and enhance your knowledge and cookery skills.

Cookery techniques

There aren't any techniques in this book that can't be done at home easily. However, there are a few techniques that you may be unfamiliar with, and these are mainly included in the Entertaining chapter. Using

these will enhance your food and create more intense flavours. Brining meat is one of these techniques; the brining process results in meat that is seasoned all the way through, rather than just on the outside. The process also tenderises the meat, so it works particularly well for tougher cuts. The only thing you need to be cautious of is not leaving the meat in the brine for too long, as this will result in meat that is too salty to be enjoyable. I have included the brining instructions within the specific recipes as the timing varies according to the type of meat used. Another technique I have used in a couple of recipes is smoking. This is not as daunting as you may expect, and there is nothing quite as satisfying as freshly smoked warm trout. I have used tea, rather than woodchips, in these recipes so you do not need to search for woodchips. It also imparts a lovely richness to the smoke flavour. I would suggest you take an old roasting dish, or even a baking tin, and dedicate it to smoking, so you don't get any smokey flavours on any other cooking you do.

For any meat cookery, you will achieve a more tender and juicy end result if you let the meat rest after cooking. Resting allows the structure of the meat to relax after it has been in the heat, enabling it to retain more of the juices. Rest it in a warm place and then give it a quick flash in the oven prior to serving.

When it comes to baking, a lighter hand is always going to achieve a better result for cakes and biscuits. Any baked item that contains gluten will get more elastic, which is the desired effect for bread, but not for cakes and biscuits.

At home

For me, cooking at home is something to be enjoyed. I hope with this book that you may also learn some interesting flavour combinations and cookery methods that you can utilise at all times, not just with my recipes from this book.

Cookery should not be viewed as scary or something that is too hard. Enjoy it and embrace it. If you make a mistake, learn from it and don't repeat it next time! Use this book, and my recipes, as a tool to move forward; they provide guidelines to allow you to develop your own style and own ideas, when you have the basic understanding of recipes and cookery techniques. Take on board what you can from my advice, and find your own way forward, in your own kitchen. Keep learning, and keep enjoying good food. Have confidence to try new things – and have fun.

MIDWEEK

Spiced cauliflower and coconut soup

This is a very easy, dairy-free soup that you can make with relatively few ingredients. The key to perfection here is to make sure you blend the soup really well until you have a velvety smooth end result.

The combination of cauliflower, spices and mellow coconut milk makes a truly delicious soup. It's lovely as a starter or as a light lunch served with some crusty sourdough with nutty olive oil.

Serves: 6
Preparation time: 10 minutes
Cooking time: 30 minutes

1 head cauliflower
3 tbsp melted coconut oil
1 onion, finely sliced
1 tsp cumin seeds, plus extra to serve
½ tsp mild curry powder, plus extra
  to serve
1 litre Vegetable Stock (page 271)
2 bay leaves
1 × 400ml tin coconut milk
handful coconut flakes, toasted, to serve
sea salt

Remove the outer leaves and tough inner core from the cauliflower. Cut the florets and stalks into small pieces.

Heat the coconut oil in a large saucepan over a medium-high heat. Add the onion, cauliflower, cumin seeds and curry powder. Sauté for 10 minutes, until the cauliflower is golden brown.

Pour in the stock and add the bay leaves. Bring to a simmer and cook for about 20 minutes until the cauliflower is tender.

Add the coconut milk and bring back to a simmer. Remove the bay leaves, then blend until you have a completely smooth soup. Season with salt to taste and serve hot, scattered with toasted coconut flakes, cumin seeds and a pinch of curry powder.

Pumpkin soup with maple-toasted seeds

I like to maximise the pumpkin flavour for this soup as much as I can by making a stock with the pumpkin skin and seeds. It makes plenty – any left over is perfect for adding to a pumpkin risotto. If you can, try to use a blue- or grey-skinned pumpkin because the flesh has a sweet, mild, refreshing flavour and vibrant orange colour, which makes the soup look amazing.

Serves: 8
Preparation time: 10 minutes
Cooking time: 1 hour 25 minutes

1 pumpkin, preferably with blue/grey
   skin, approx. 2kg
1 bay leaf
1 sprig of rosemary
125g butter
1 tsp sea salt
250ml milk
sea salt and freshly ground black pepper

FOR THE MAPLE-TOASTED SEEDS
60g pumpkin seeds
1 tbsp maple syrup
½ tbsp olive oil, plus extra to serve
¼ tsp sea salt

Peel and quarter the pumpkin, reserving the skin and seeds. Cut the pumpkin flesh into rough 2cm chunks, and set aside. Put the skin, seeds, trimmings, bay leaf and rosemary in a large saucepan. Cover with about 2.5 litres water, bring to the boil and simmer for 1 hour. Strain and reserve the stock.

While the stock is simmering, preheat the oven to 200°C/180°C fan/gas 6. To make the seeds, mix together the pumpkin seeds, maple syrup, olive oil and ¼ teaspoon of salt. Scatter evenly on a baking tray and bake for 8–10 minutes, until golden. Remove and allow to cool, then roughly chop.

Melt the butter in a large saucepan over medium heat, and add the pumpkin chunks and 1 teaspoon of salt. Cook for about 5 minutes, until the pumpkin starts to soften.

Pour in about half of the pumpkin stock and bring to a simmer. Cook for 10 minutes, until the pumpkin is completely soft and starting to break down. Stir in the milk, remove the rosemary sprig and bay leaf. Using a stick blender (or transfer to a food processor), blitz until completely smooth, adding more stock as required. Season to taste.

Serve the soup hot, scattered with the maple-toasted pumpkin seeds and drizzled with oil.

Minestrone soup

This is often a go-to recipe after the weekend in which I can use up a few of the veggies left in the fridge, simply chopped up and sautéed with bacon. You don't have to be too precise with quantities here — it's supposed to be a rustic soup that's colourful and full of flavour.

Serves: 4–6
Preparation time: 20 minutes
Cooking time: 25–30 minutes

2 tbsp olive oil
1 small onion, finely chopped
1 celery stick, finely chopped
1 leek, finely chopped
1 carrot, finely diced
2 rashers streaky bacon, cut into thin
   strips
1 small potato, finely diced
¼ medium-large Savoy cabbage, finely
   shredded
2 tbsp tomato purée
1 × 400g tin haricot beans, drained and
   rinsed
1 sprig of thyme
1 sprig of rosemary
1.5 litres Chicken Stock (page 270)
75–100g dried pasta such as orzo,
   broken spaghetti or macaroni
175g green beans, each cut into thirds
handful of flat-leaf parsley, chopped
sea salt and freshly ground black pepper
freshly grated Parmesan cheese, to serve
crème fraîche, to serve (optional)

Heat the olive oil in a large saucepan and add the onion, celery, leek, carrot and bacon. Fry over medium heat until the bacon starts to brown and the vegetables soften.

Add the potato, cabbage, tomato purée, beans and herbs. Season with salt and pepper. Continue to cook for a couple of minutes, add the stock, then bring to the boil.

Stir in the pasta and cook for 5 minutes, then add the green beans and continue to cook until the pasta is tender.

Taste, adding a little more seasoning if you like, then stir in the parsley. Serve with a sprinkle of Parmesan and a blob of crème fraîche, if you like.

Field mushroom and thyme soup

If you like mushrooms, you'll love this soup. To really intensify the flavour of the mushrooms, cook them until they reduce in size and any moisture they contain has been released. The addition of mascarpone to this soup lends it a rich creaminess, while the sherry vinegar gives a little bite, lifting the end result.

Serves: 6
Preparation time: 10 minutes
Cooking time: 25 minutes

50g butter
1 onion, sliced
1 garlic clove, crushed
½ bunch of thyme, plus extra picked
　leaves to serve
1 bay leaf
1kg field (flat) mushrooms, sliced
1 litre Chicken or Vegetable Stock (pages
　270–1)
250ml whole milk
1 tbsp sherry vinegar
sea salt and freshly ground black pepper
6 tbsp mascarpone cheese, to serve

Melt the butter in a large wide saucepan until it starts to become frothy. Add the onion, garlic, thyme and bay leaf. Season well with salt and pepper. Cook over medium heat for up to 10 minutes, until the onion is golden and caramelised.

Add the mushrooms and cook for 15–20 minutes, until any liquid that seeps out has almost cooked away. Add 75ml stock and all of the milk. Bring to simmer and cook for 10 minutes.

Remove the thyme stalks and bay leaf. Purée until smooth, adding more stock if required. Stir in the sherry vinegar and add a little more seasoning if you like.

Spoon into bowls and serve with a dollop of mascarpone cheese and a few picked thyme leaves scattered over.

Chicken and asparagus salad with crispy chicken skin

Less really is more in this recipe, which has only the minimum of ingredients. It works well served as a light lunch or dinner in the summer months – I'll often throw a few boiled new potatoes on the side to make it more substantial.

Buy free-range, corn-fed chicken breasts if possible, because they have a far richer flavour and texture, which really comes through when they are poached. Make sure you get them with the skin on, as the best part about this salad is the crisp, salty chicken skin – it really shouldn't be missed out on.

Serves: 4
Preparation time: 20 minutes, plus 24 hours chilling
Cooking time: 20 minutes

4 skin-on chicken breasts
2 tsp sea salt, plus extra for seasoning
50g butter
2 bunches of asparagus, tough ends trimmed and sliced in half diagonally
finely grated zest and juice of ½ lemon
4 tbsp extra virgin olive oil
freshly ground black pepper
4 tbsp picked marjoram leaves

FOR THE BRINE
85g sea salt
2 tsp white peppercorns
2 tsp coriander seeds
2 tsp fennel seeds
2 bay leaves
few sprigs of thyme

To make the brine, put all of the brine ingredients in a medium-large saucepan, pour in 1.25 litres of cold water and bring to the boil. Remove from the heat and leave to cool. When cold add the chicken breasts and leave them in the brine for 24 hours in the fridge. Remove the chicken from the brine, rinse under cold water and pat dry.

Preheat the oven to 200°C/180°C fan/gas 6. Line a baking sheet with baking parchment. Use a sharp knife to carefully remove the chicken skin and spread out on the prepared baking sheet. Sprinkle over the salt. Top with another piece of parchment and sit a baking sheet on top (this will help to hold the chicken skin flat). Put in the oven for 15–20 minutes until the skin is golden and crisp. Remove and leave the crispy chicken skin to cool before breaking into shards.

Smother the brined chicken breasts in the butter and season with salt. Wrap each one tightly in clingfilm. Bring a saucepan of water to the boil and add the chicken. Turn down the heat to a gentle simmer. Poach gently for 12–16 minutes (depending on the size of the chicken breasts). Cool slightly, then chill in the fridge.

Bring a separate pan of salted water to the boil. Blanch the asparagus for a couple of minutes and refresh in ice-cold water to stop it cooking any further. Then mix the lemon zest and juice with the extra virgin olive oil. Season with salt and black pepper.

Remove the chicken from the clingfilm and wipe away any butter. Thinly slice and arrange between serving plates. Cut the asparagus spears into three and add to the plate with the marjoram. Spoon over the dressing and finish topped with the crispy chicken skin and salt and pepper.

Beetroot salad with spelt and toasted walnuts

This salad has a wonderful colour, texture and, above all, taste.

Serves: 4
Preparation time: 20 minutes
Cooking time: about 1 hour

150g spelt
4 raw beetroots
50ml red wine vinegar
2 tbsp olive oil
50g walnut pieces
30g porridge oats
¼ tsp ground cinnamon
½ tsp soft brown sugar
2 tsp chopped tarragon leaves, plus
    extra to serve
sea salt and freshly ground black pepper
salad cress, to serve

FOR THE VINAIGRETTE
25ml white wine vinegar
1 tsp sweet sherry
50ml walnut oil
50ml olive oil
½ tsp Dijon mustard
½ tsp wholegrain mustard

Cook the spelt according to the packet instructions, drain and allow to cool.

Put the beetroots in a saucepan and cover with water. Add the salt and red wine vinegar. Bring to the boil and cook for about 1 hour, or until just tender. Leave to cool, then peel and cut each one into 4–6 wedges, drizzle with 1 tablespoon of olive oil and season with salt and pepper. Set aside.

Heat a medium-large frying pan and add the walnuts. Move around in the pan to toast. Remove and roughly chop.

Return the pan to the heat and add the remaining 1 tablespoon of olive oil. When hot, scatter in the oats and toss around in the pan until light golden in colour. Sprinkle over the cinnamon and sugar, toss around to coat the oats and remove from the pan to cool.

To make the vinaigrette, whisk all of the ingredients together and season to taste with salt and pepper.

To assemble the salad, mix together the spelt, tarragon, walnuts and 4 tablespoons of vinaigrette. Place the spelt on a plate and sprinkle over the toasted oats. Add the wedges of beetroot and scatter with the tarragon and salad cress. Drizzle with extra dressing and serve straight away.

Sweet potato, quinoa, green bean and peanut salad with buttermilk dressing

You know this salad will be good for you just by looking at the ingredients list. Serve this alone for a light lunch or alongside some grilled chicken or fish for a healthy midweek meal.

Serves: 4–6
Preparation time: 15 minutes
Cooking time: 30 minutes

2 large sweet potatoes, scrubbed and cut into 2cm chunks
2 tbsp vegetable oil
1 sprig of rosemary, leaves picked
5 garlic cloves, crushed with the back of a knife
pinch of sea salt, plus extra to season
50g raw unsalted peanuts
100g quinoa
200g green beans
freshly ground black pepper

FOR THE DRESSING
150ml buttermilk
finely grated zest of 1 lime
2cm piece of fresh ginger, peeled and grated
bunch of coriander, chopped
2 tbsp honey

Preheat the oven to 180°C/160°C fan/gas 5.

Arrange the sweet potato chunks on a roasting tray, drizzle over the vegetable oil and scatter with the rosemary leaves, garlic and salt. Toss to coat well in the oil and bake in the oven for 25–30 minutes, until the potatoes are lightly golden and cooked through. Leave to cool.

While the potatoes are cooking, put the peanuts on a small baking tray and roast in the oven for 10–12 minutes, until golden. Cool slightly, then roughly chop.

Put the quinoa and enough water to cover it in a saucepan, place over high heat and bring to the boil. Boil for 1 minute, reduce the heat to low and cover and cook for 12 minutes. Remove from the heat and leave to sit with the lid on for a further 5 minutes. Fork through the quinoa to separate the grains and leave to cool.

Bring a saucepan of salted water to the boil and cook the green beans for 3 minutes, until just tender. Drain and refresh in cold water.

To make the dressing, mix together the dressing ingredients and season to taste.

Put the cooled sweet potato, quinoa and green beans in a large bowl and gently mix in the dressing. Scatter over the chopped peanuts and serve at room temperature.

Spicy summer rice salad

You can quite easily make this using white rice, but the nuttiness of the brown basmati and firm texture of the wild rice really turn this simple salad into something quite special. If you want to make this a more balanced meal, flake in some smoked mackerel or even pan-fry fresh mackerel fillets to serve alongside. One tip here is to make sure you leave the salad to stand for a good half an hour or so before serving, then all the flavours will marry together beautifully.

Serves: 4
Preparation time: 30 minutes
Cooking time: approx. 25 minutes

150g mixed brown basmati and wild rice
½ cucumber, halved, seeds removed and
    finely chopped
6–8 radishes, finely chopped
1 red pepper, deseeded and finely
    chopped
1 red chilli, deseeded and finely chopped
large handful of coriander leaves,
    chopped
sea salt and freshly ground black pepper

FOR THE DRESSING
5 tbsp lemon juice
3 tbsp olive oil
1 tbsp sesame oil
2 tbsp soy sauce

Cook the rice according to the packet instructions. Drain well and leave to cool in a large bowl.

Add the cucumber, radishes, red pepper and chilli to the rice and mix together.

Whisk together all of the ingredients for the dressing and season with salt and pepper.

Pour over the salad and gently mix to combine. Cover and chill in the fridge for at least 30 minutes for the flavours to come together.

When you are ready to serve, toss in the chopped coriander and add a little more seasoning if you like.

Summer feta salad

If I ever need a reminder of family summer holidays, this salad will always do the trick. The key here is to allow plenty of time for the onion, tomatoes and fennel to marinate, as this will ensure you get the best flavour from them.

This salad works perfectly well as a standalone dish served with plenty of crusty bread to mop up the juices. However, I also like to serve it alongside other salads and some barbecued fish or meat when I'm cooking for larger groups.

Serves: 4–6
Preparation time: 30 minutes, plus
   1 hour marinating

1 red onion, finely sliced
1 tsp dried oregano
100ml red wine vinegar
5 large ripe tomatoes
1 tsp caster sugar
juice of ½ lemon
1 fennel bulb, finely sliced
1 romaine or cos lettuce
300–400g feta cheese
125g pitted black Kalamata olives,
   chopped
large handful of flat-leaf parsley,
   chopped
sea salt and freshly ground black pepper
crusty bread, to serve

First of all the onion, tomatoes and fennel need to be prepared and set aside for about 1 hour. Put the onion in a bowl. Stir in the oregano and red wine vinegar and season with salt and pepper. Cover with clingfilm and set aside to marinate for at least 1 hour.

Cut the tomatoes into chunks, then sprinkle over the caster sugar and a good pinch of salt. Set aside.

Squeeze the lemon juice over the fennel, add a pinch of salt and about 1 tablespoon of the red wine vinegar from the onion bowl and set aside.

When you are ready to assemble the salad, cut or tear the lettuce leaves into large pieces and put in a large salad bowl. Cut or crumble the feta into about 1cm chunks and scatter over the lettuce. Add the olives, parsley and onions along with all of the marinating vinegar, tomatoes and fennel. Gently fold together and add a little more seasoning if you like.

Serve straight away with crusty bread.

Braised chicken legs with Puy lentils and tomato

If you find you have some midweek entertaining to do, this chicken dish is ideal. You cook the whole recipe in one pan, and even though it looks like there are a lot of ingredients, the preparation and cooking part of the recipe are pretty straight-forward. It's your cooker that does most of the hard work!

Serves: 4
Preparation time: 15 minutes
Cooking time: 1 hour 15 minutes

2 tbsp cornflour
4 chicken legs
2 tbsp olive oil
20g butter
1 tsp cumin seeds
1 tsp fennel seeds
1 tsp coriander seeds
1 tsp nigella seeds
2 garlic cloves, crushed
1 onion, finely chopped
1 celery stick, finely chopped
1 large carrot, finely chopped
2 bay leaves
2 sprigs of thyme
150ml Madeira wine
200ml white wine
2 tbsp tomato purée
850ml Chicken Stock (page 270)
250g Puy lentils
150g semi-dried tomatoes, roughly
   chopped
sea salt and freshly ground black pepper
2 tbsp chopped flat-leaf parsley, to serve

In a bowl, mix the cornflour with some salt and pepper and add the chicken legs. Coat well and set aside.

Heat the olive oil and the butter in a large, wide, ovenproof saucepan over medium heat. Add the chicken and brown for about 10 minutes until the skin is evenly golden.

Lightly crush the seeds in a pestle and mortar. Remove the chicken from the pan and add the garlic, onion, celery, carrot, bay leaves, thyme sprigs and the crushed seeds. Cook for about 10 minutes over medium-low heat, until the vegetables are softened.

Preheat the oven to 180°C/160°C fan/gas 4.

Turn up the heat under the pan and pour in the Madeira and white wine. Bring to the boil and allow to bubble away until reduced by half.

Stir in the tomato purée and chicken stock. Return to the boil, add the lentils and return the chicken to the pan. Cover with a lid and put in the oven for 30 minutes.

Remove from the oven, stir through the tomatoes and then continue to cook in the oven, uncovered, for a further 15 minutes. Remove the thyme stalks and bay leaves and scatter over the parsley to serve.

Chicken curry korma-style

This has become a real favourite in my house and we really go to town with the accompaniments – plain rice, poppadoms, dried chilli flakes for added heat, a dollop of crème fraîche, steamed greens and a tangy mango chutney – bought or, if time allows, homemade (see page 275). You'll have plenty of paste for two curries here, so store the extra in the fridge ready for a quick meal another day. You can, of course, use a bought paste, but it really is well worth making your own. *(See image on previous pages.)*

Serves: 4
Preparation time: 25 minutes, plus at
 least 2 hours marinating
Cooking time: 25 minutes

FOR THE MARINADE
4 skinless chicken breasts or 500g
 skinless and boneless thighs, cut into
 2.5cm chunks
100ml groundnut or olive oil
3 garlic cloves, crushed
1cm piece of fresh ginger, peeled and
 grated
freshly ground black pepper

FOR THE CURRY PASTE
1 tsp ground cumin
1 tsp ground coriander
1 tsp chilli powder
1 tsp ground turmeric
1 tsp garam masala
pinch of flaked sea salt
1 garlic clove, crushed
1cm piece of fresh ginger, peeled and
 chopped
50g ground almonds

Put the chicken in a bowl with the 100ml oil, garlic, ginger and a few turns of freshly ground black pepper. Cover and set aside in the fridge for a couple of hours, or overnight if time allows.

To make the paste, pound all the spices together in a pestle and mortar with a good pinch of flaked sea salt, the garlic and ginger. Once combined, stir in the ground almonds and 100ml of water.

To make the curry sauce, heat a large saucepan over medium-high heat and add the 2 tablespoons of groundnut oil. Once hot, add the onion, celery, carrot, garlic, cinnamon and cardamom and sauté for 5 minutes until the onion is softened but not coloured.

Stir in about 4 tablespoons of the curry paste and cook for a couple of minutes to bring out all the spice flavours. (Put the remaining paste in the fridge to use another day.)

Pour in the wine and let it bubble until it has reduced down. Slowly add the coconut milk, stirring to blend into the curry paste. Add the fish sauce, reduce the heat to medium-low and simmer for about 10 minutes, until the carrot is tender.

Meanwhile, heat a large frying pan over high heat. Remove the chicken from the marinade, shaking off the excess oil, and add the pieces to the hot pan. (Depending on the size of your pan you may need to do this in batches to avoid overcrowding.) Quickly brown the chicken on both sides.

FOR THE CURRY SAUCE
2 tbsp groundnut oil
1 onion, finely chopped
1 celery stick, finely chopped
1 carrot, finely diced
1 garlic clove, crushed
1 cinnamon stick
4 cardamom pods, crushed
100ml white wine
1 × 400ml tin coconut milk
1 tbsp fish sauce
handful of chopped coriander, plus
    extra sprigs to serve
plain yoghurt, to serve
Mango Chutney (page 275), to serve

Once the chicken is browned all over, add to the sauce. Simmer for about 5 minutes for the chicken to cook through and take on the flavours. Taste and season with more salt if you like. To finish, remove the cinnamon stick and cardamom pods, and stir through the coriander. Serve with Steamed Aromatic Basmati Rice (below), a dollop of yoghurt and coriander sprinkled on top with Mango Chutney on the side.

Steamed aromatic basmati rice

Serves: 4
Preparation time: 10 minutes, plus
    30 minutes soaking
Cooking time: 15 minutes

250g pure basmati rice
1 tsp sea salt
1 cinnamon stick
1 tsp whole cloves
1 tsp cardamom pods, lightly crushed
    with the back of a spoon

Put the rice into a large bowl. Fill with cold water and swill with your hand. Immediately tip out the cloudy water, leaving the wet grains behind. Repeat 3–4 times and the water will become less cloudy. Cover with water once more and leave the rice to soak for up to 30 minutes. Drain the grains in a sieve and tip into a medium-large saucepan.

Add 600ml fresh cold water, the salt and the spices. Place the pan over high heat, bring to the boil and cover immediately with a tight-fitting lid. Turn the heat to low and leave to cook for 10 minutes – resist the temptation to lift off the lid.

After 10 minutes, turn off the heat, keeping the lid firmly in place, and leave to stand for 5 minutes.

Run a fork through the rice to separate the grains, remove the cinnamon stick and serve with the curry.

Chorizo chicken

Next time you are short of an idea for what to do with that chicken breast, give this a try. It's full of rich, robust flavours and colour. I highly recommend serving it with the most delicious Polenta Chips (see page 54) and some steamed green beans.

Serves: 4
Preparation time: 20 minutes
Cooking time: 20 minutes

125g cooking chorizo
½ small red onion, very finely chopped
3 tbsp white breadcrumbs
1 egg, beaten
2 tsp finely chopped fresh oregano or
  1 tsp dried oregano
grated zest of ½ lemon
4 skin-on and bone-in chicken breasts
olive oil, for drizzling
sea salt and freshly ground black pepper
Romesco Sauce (page 276), to serve

Preheat the oven to 200°C/180°C fan/gas 6.

Remove the skin/casing from the chorizo and chop finely. Mix the chorizo, onion, breadcrumbs, egg, oregano and lemon zest together in a bowl.

Make a pocket between the skin and meat of the chicken breasts, making sure the skin stays attached at the sides. Stuff each breast with the chorizo mixture and, using your fingers, press to spread over the top of the meat. If the skin becomes detached, use a cocktail stick to secure it.

Place on a lightly oiled baking tray. Drizzle a little olive oil over the top of the chicken and season with salt and pepper. Cook in the oven for 20 minutes, until the skin is golden and crisp and the chicken just cooked through.

Leave the cooked chicken to rest for 5 minutes before serving with the Romesco Sauce (page 276).

Jane's sweet and sour-style chicken

As with many of my meat dishes, I recommend you leave the chicken to marinate for as long as possible to give a really tender, flavoursome end result. Here I suggest leaving the chicken breast in the ginger, garlic and oil for up to 48 hours, so make sure you plan ahead for when you want to cook this dish.

Serves: 4
Preparation time: 20 minutes, plus
   1–48 hours marinating
Cooking time: 1 hour

1cm piece of fresh ginger, peeled and
   grated
1 garlic clove, crushed
100ml sesame oil
4 skinless chicken breasts, cut into large
   chunks
approx. 100ml olive oil

FOR THE SAUCE
2 tbsp olive oil
1 onion, chopped
1 celery stick, chopped
1 garlic clove, crushed
1 carrot, finely diced
1 red pepper, deseeded and finely diced
1 tbsp plain flour
2 tbsp Chinese wine or sherry
1 × 432g tin pineapple pieces, in juice
2 tbsp Branston Pickle
1 tbsp soy sauce
1 tbsp Worcestershire sauce
1 tbsp tomato ketchup
2 tbsp light brown sugar
2 tbsp malt vinegar
1 tbsp fish sauce
1 large courgette, diced

In a large shallow bowl, mix together the ginger, garlic and sesame oil. Add the chicken to the bowl. Pour over enough olive oil to make sure the chicken is covered, then stir to coat the chicken in the marinade. Cover and keep in the fridge to marinate for a minimum of 1 hour or up to 48 hours if time allows.

To make the sauce, heat the olive oil in a large pan over medium heat and gently fry the onion, celery and garlic until soft but not coloured. Add the carrot and red pepper and cook for a couple of minutes.

Add the flour and stir it around in the pan to prevent it from catching, and cook for a further minute. Pour in the wine or sherry, stir with a wooden spoon to deglaze, loosening and incorporating any sediment from the bottom of the pan. Drain in the pineapple juice, reserving the pieces for later.

Add all of the remaining sauce ingredients, apart from the pineapple pieces and courgette, and add 100ml of hot water. Stir well, cover and simmer for 30 minutes, topping up with extra water if needed. The sauce should be thick enough to coat the cooked chicken.

While the sauce is cooking, heat a large frying pan over medium heat. Remove the chicken from the marinade and drain off the excess oil. Add the pieces to the pan, in a couple batches if needed, making sure the chicken browns rather than steams.

Add the browned chicken to the sauce along with the diced courgette and reserved pineapple pieces. Continue to cook, uncovered, for a further 10 minutes.

Aromatic winter duck, red cabbage and plums

The key to a good stir-fry is to avoid overcrowding the wok or pan, otherwise the vegetables will steam and become soggy rather than retain their crunch. As for the duck, slow-cooking the skin side will give you a lovely crisp texture while ensuring the fat has been cooked out.

Serves: 2
Preparation time: 15 minutes
Cooking time: 15–18 minutes

2 duck breasts, skin on
2 tsp Chinese five-spice powder
pinch of sea salt
1 tbsp groundnut oil
4 ripe plums, quartered and stone
   removed
1 tbsp honey
splash of soy sauce
75ml orange juice
4 tsp sesame oil
1cm piece of fresh ginger, peeled and
   grated
2 garlic cloves, peeled and crushed
½ red chilli, deseeded and finely chopped
½ small red cabbage, finely shredded
1 small red onion, finely sliced
100g sugar snap peas
1 tbsp toasted sesame seeds

Score the skin of the duck several times with a sharp knife and put in a bowl. Add the five-spice, a good pinch of salt and groundnut oil, and rub into the duck.

Put the duck, skin-side down, in a cold non-stick frying pan and place over medium-high heat. Once the fat starts to be released from the skin, tilt the pan and occasionally remove with a spoon (this can be reserved to use for cooking another time). Cook for about 6 minutes until the skin is golden and crisp. Turn over and cook for 5 minutes. Remove from the pan and leave the duck to rest.

Drain away any excess fat from the pan, turn the heat to high and add the plums. Cook for a minute or so on each cut side until golden. Add the honey, a splash of soy sauce and 2 tablespoons of the orange juice. Toss to coat in the sticky sauce and remove from the heat.

Heat a wok over a high heat with the sesame oil. Fry the ginger, garlic and chilli for 30 seconds before adding the cabbage and onion. Stir-fry for 3–4 minutes until the vegetables begin to soften. Add the sugar snap peas, another splash of soy sauce and the remaining orange juice. Toss around for a minute or so until the vegetables are tender but still a little crunchy.

Arrange the duck (sliced first, if preferred) and plums on plates, spooning any juices over the plums. Place the stir-fry to the side and sprinkle with toasted sesame seeds.

Pasta and courgette carbonara

The idea for this dish originally came from wanting to get my kids to eat more vegetables. It's the perfect recipe to get fussy eaters to eat courgette. The key here is to make sure you don't overcook the egg, otherwise it will scramble and you miss out on the rich creamy sauce that carbonara is known for. To do this, as soon as you add the egg to the pasta, remove the pan from the heat.

Serves: 2
Preparation time: 10 minutes
Cooking time: 15 minutes

150g dried spaghetti or linguine
olive oil
75g diced pancetta or 2 rashers bacon, finely chopped
2 eggs
4 tbsp crème fraîche
1 courgette, grated
25g grated Parmesan cheese, plus extra to serve
1 small onion, finely sliced
1 garlic clove, chopped
handful of button mushrooms, halved or quartered, depending on their size
100ml white wine
handful of small basil leaves, to serve
sea salt and freshly ground black pepper

Bring a medium-large saucepan of salted water to the boil. Cook the pasta for about 10 minutes, until al dente. Drain and return to the pan, tossing with a little olive oil.

Heat a large saucepan over medium heat and add the pancetta. Fry until it becomes light golden brown and the fat has rendered. If using rashers of bacon you may need a drop of olive oil to prevent sticking.

Meanwhile, beat together the eggs and crème fraîche. Stir in the courgette and Parmesan cheese. Set aside.

Add the onion and garlic to the pancetta, fry for a few minutes to soften, then stir in the mushrooms. Cook for a further 5 minutes, until the mushrooms are tender and becoming golden. Pour in the white wine, cook for a few moments and season with salt and pepper.

Tip the cooked pasta into the pan and toss around to heat through. Add the egg mix and grated courgette and season to taste with salt and pepper. Mix around to combine, then remove from the heat. The heat from the pasta and the pan will cook the eggs, which will thicken and cling to the pasta without becoming overcooked. Serve straight away with extra Parmesan cheese and the basil leaves sprinkled over.

Family hot dog and bacon pasta

My ideal way to serve this dish is in a large bowl, scattered with plenty of cheese and placed in the middle of the table for all the family to help themselves to. A simple salad and garlic bread served alongside is a must for a fun family supper.

Serves: 4
Preparation time: 20 minutes
Cooking time: 30 minutes

1 tbsp olive oil, plus extra for drizzling
2–3 rashers of streaky bacon, diced, or 70g diced pancetta
1 small onion, finely chopped
1 garlic clove, crushed
125g baby chestnut or button mushrooms, halved
10 Frankfurter sausages, cut into 2.5cm pieces
good splash of red or white wine
1 × 400g tin chopped tomatoes
handful of basil leaves, roughly chopped
1 small-medium courgette, diced (optional)
400g fresh pasta shapes, such as penne
6–8 artichoke hearts in oil, drained and quartered (optional)
sea salt and freshly ground black pepper
grated Parmesan or Cheddar cheese, to serve

Heat the olive oil in a large high-sided frying pan over medium heat, add the bacon and cook until starting to brown. Stir in the onion, garlic, mushrooms and Frankfurter pieces and cook until the onion is starting to soften and brown, stirring continuously to prevent it sticking to the pan.

Pour in a splash of wine, stir with a wooden spoon to deglaze, loosening and incorporating any sediment from the bottom of the pan. Stir in the chopped tomatoes, half a tin of water (approximately 200ml), the basil and courgette, if using. Bring to a simmer and cook for about 10 minutes to reduce the sauce and cook the courgette.

Meanwhile, cook the pasta in boiling salted water according to the packet instructions.

Season the sauce with salt and pepper and then stir in the artichokes, if using.

Drain the pasta, drizzle with olive oil and season, then divide between plates. Serve the sauce spooned over the top, with plenty of cheese to scatter over.

Wareing family lasagne

I think every home needs a family lasagne recipe, and this is one that has developed and improved over the years until it has now become a staple in the Wareing household. It's not a quick dish to make, so we will quite often double up the recipe and put one in the freezer. (*See images on following pages.*)

Serves: 6–8
Preparation time: 20 minutes
Cooking time: 1 hour 50 minutes
   (including cooking the meat sauce)

1 tbsp olive oil
1kg minced beef or lamb
1 large onion, chopped
2 garlic cloves, chopped
2 celery sticks, chopped
1 tsp flaked sea salt
½ tsp freshly ground black pepper
½ tsp cayenne pepper
300ml red wine
2 × 400g tins chopped tomatoes
2 tbsp tomato ketchup
2 tbsp tomato purée
1 tbsp Worcestershire sauce
1 tbsp brown sauce
500ml strong Beef Stock (page 270)
3 bay leaves
2 sprigs each of thyme and rosemary
handful of basil leaves, chopped
12–14 sheets dried egg lasagne
250g buffalo mozzarella, sliced
100g Cheddar cheese, grated

FOR THE WHITE SAUCE
600ml milk
1 small onion, peeled but left whole
10 cloves
1 bay leaf
50g butter
50g plain flour
sea salt and freshly ground black pepper

To make the meat sauce, heat the olive oil in a large saucepan. Add the mince and fry to brown all over, breaking up any chunks with a wooden spoon. Stir in the onion, garlic and celery, and continue to fry until the onion softens. Season with the salt, black pepper and the cayenne pepper.

Pour the wine into the pan and bring to the boil, allowing it to reduce completely. Stir in the tomatoes, ketchup, tomato purée, Worcestershire sauce, brown sauce, stock and herbs. Bring to a simmer, cover and cook gently for up to 1 hour. Once cooked, add a little more seasoning if you like and remove the bay leaves and thyme and rosemary sprigs.

Meanwhile, make the white sauce. Put the milk in a small saucepan. Stud the onion with the cloves and add it to the milk along with the bay leaf. Gently bring to the boil over low heat. Remove from the heat and leave to infuse for a few minutes before removing the bay leaf and onion.

Melt the butter in a saucepan and add the flour, salt and pepper. Cook over low heat for about 1 minute to get rid of the floury taste but avoid letting it brown. Add a ladle of the infused milk and stir to combine. Continue adding the milk a little at a time until you have a thick pouring sauce. Keep hot, over a low heat.

Preheat the oven to 180°C/160°C fan/gas 5. To assemble the lasagne, put a layer of meat sauce in the base of a large ovenproof dish (approximately 20cm square, 8cm deep). Sit a layer of pasta on top, pour over a layer of white sauce and dot with a few slices of mozzarella. Continue with the same process using three layers of pasta and finishing with a layer of white sauce and mozzarella. Finally, scatter with Cheddar, sit the dish on a baking tray and bake for about 40 minutes, until the top is golden brown.

Herb-marinated lamb steaks with Mediterranean stew

For a tasty end result, make sure you allow plenty of marinating time for the lamb steaks in this recipe. These are a really quick-cooking cut of meat, but if they are marinated first the flesh remains beautifully tender.

Serves: 4
Preparation time: 20 minutes, plus up to 48 hours marinating
Cooking time: 20 minutes

4 lamb leg steaks
100ml olive oil
4 peeled strips of lemon zest
2 tsp fennel seeds, lightly crushed
1 tsp coriander seeds, lightly crushed
2 garlic cloves, lightly crushed
½ bunch of thyme
2 sprigs of rosemary

FOR THE STEW
2 tbsp olive oil
1 red pepper, deseeded and cut into 1cm dice
1 yellow pepper, deseeded and cut into 1cm dice
1 courgette, cut into 1cm dice
1 aubergine, cut into 1cm dice
2 garlic cloves
2 tsp fresh thyme leaves
1 tsp hot paprika
500ml tomato passata
small handful of basil leaves, finely chopped
sea salt and freshly ground black pepper

Put the lamb steaks in a shallow bowl and mix with the 100ml of olive oil, the lemon zest, fennel and coriander seeds, the garlic, thyme and rosemary. Cover and leave to marinate in the fridge for up to 48 hours.

For the stew, heat the olive oil in a saucepan over medium-low heat and cook the peppers for 5 minutes, until softened. Add the courgette, aubergine, garlic, thyme and paprika and continue to cook for 5 minutes until the vegetables are just tender. Stir in the tomato passata and season with salt and pepper. Bring to a simmer and cook for 10 minutes, stirring occasionally.

Meanwhile, to cook the lamb, remove it from the marinade and wipe off any excess oil. Heat a large frying pan over high heat and cook the steaks for 1–2 minutes, each side, depending on the thickness. Remove from the pan and leave to rest for 5 minutes.

While the steaks are resting, fry the reserved marinade in a large pan until crispy.

Stir the basil into the stew and serve with the rested lamb along with any resting juices and the fried marinade sprinkled on top.

Griddled lamb chops with green beans, mint and shallot

Cooking lamb chops on the griddle is the perfect way to prepare them; the meat stays juicy and tender and the fat runs into the grooves of the pan.

In my opinion, mint and green beans are a great flavour match for lamb, so I've created this tangy chutney to serve alongside, making this a lovely midweek supper. Buttered new potatoes or some mash would also not go amiss.

Serves: 4
Preparation time: 30 minutes
Cooking time: 25 minutes

250g fine green beans
8 loin lamb chops
olive oil, for brushing
sea salt and freshly ground black pepper

FOR THE MINT PURÉE
30g fresh mint, leaves picked
3 garlic cloves, 2 roughly chopped and
  1 left whole
50ml rapeseed oil

FOR THE SHALLOT CHUTNEY
3 large banana shallots, chopped
200ml malt vinegar, plus 1 tbsp
50g capers
30g caster sugar
2 tsp nigella seeds

To make the mint mixture, bring a pan of water to the boil. Blanch the mint leaves and roughly chopped garlic for 30 seconds. Drain and refresh in ice-cold water. Put in a mini blender and blitz to a smooth purée while adding the oil. Once done, finely grate the whole garlic into it (ideally, use a Microplane grater) and stir through. Season and set aside.

To prepare the beans, blanch them in a pan of boiling water for 4 minutes and refresh in ice-cold water. Drain and finely chop. Add to the mint purée, mix together and set aside.

To make the shallot chutney, put the shallots, 200ml vinegar, capers, caster sugar, nigella seeds and 75ml of water in a saucepan. Bring to the boil and allow to reduce until there is no liquid remaining. Stir in the remaining 1 tablespoon of vinegar and set aside.

Heat a griddle pan over high heat until very hot. Brush the lamb chops all over with a little olive oil and season with salt and pepper. Sit the chops fat-side down on the griddle, leaning them up against each other for support. Cook for 4–5 minutes until the fat renders and becomes crisp.

Lay the chops flat on their sides and cook for 4–5 minutes each side, basting with the rendered fat. Remove and allow the chops to rest for 5 minutes.

Add a little more seasoning to the bean and mint mixture if you like, then spoon on to plates with the rested lamb chops. Drizzle the shallot chutney over the top.

Homemade beef burger

For this recipe, ask your butcher to mince some chuck steak for you, as it really will give a far superior result than standard pre-packaged beef mince. If this isn't an option, pulse some diced chuck steak in a food processor until finely chopped.

Makes: 4
Preparation time: 20 minutes
Cooking time: 20 minutes

20g butter
1 onion, finely chopped
1 garlic clove, crushed
600g minced chuck steak
8 rashers smoked streaky bacon, finely
   diced or minced
1 egg, lightly beaten
1 tsp sea salt, plus extra to season
½ tsp freshly ground black pepper, plus
   extra to season
olive oil, for frying

TO SERVE
4 tsp English mustard
200g sliced Monterey Jack cheese
8 rashers smoked streaky bacon
4 brioche burger buns, split in half
4 tbsp tomato ketchup
1 large ripe beef tomato, sliced

Heat the butter in a saucepan and gently sauté the onion and garlic until softened but not coloured. Transfer to a large bowl and leave to cool.

When cool, add the minced steak, bacon, egg, salt and pepper and mix well. Heat a frying pan and fry a small amount of the mixture in a little oil and add a little more seasoning, if you like.

Shape the mixture into four burgers and either chill in the fridge or cook straight away.

Preheat the oven to 180°C/160°C fan/gas 4. Heat the olive oil in a large frying pan set over high heat. Fry the burgers for a minute or so on each side, until browned. Sit on a baking tray and brush each one with the mustard and top with cheese. Bake for 6 minutes for medium-rare. Increase the cooking time if you prefer well done.

Meanwhile, grill the bacon until crisp and lightly toast the brioche buns. As soon as the burgers are ready, assemble together with some tomato ketchup and sliced beef tomato, and season with salt and pepper.

Chilli minced beef with smoked paprika butter

A simple chilli con carne is a very useful recipe to have in your repertoire, but this recipe goes one step further with the addition of the rather special butter. Stir it through just before serving; the paprika will add a rich smokiness and the lime a tangy lift.

Serves: 6
Preparation time: 10 minutes
Cooking time: 1 hour 15 minutes–
   2 hours 15 minutes

2 tbsp garlic oil or olive oil
2 onions, thinly sliced
2 celery sticks, chopped
2 garlic cloves, chopped
1kg lean minced beef
200ml red wine
2 × 400g tins kidney beans, or 350g
   dried kidney beans soaked in water
   overnight, drained
1 × 400g tin whole tomatoes
1 red chilli, finely chopped or 2 tsp chilli
   powder
1 tsp crushed cumin seeds
500ml strong Beef Stock (page 270)
2 bay leaves
4 sprigs of thyme
2 sprigs of rosemary
1 tsp flaked sea salt
freshly ground black pepper
large handful of chopped coriander
   leaves, plus extra sprigs to serve
lime wedges, to serve

FOR THE SMOKED PAPRIKA BUTTER
75g soft butter
1½ tsp smoked paprika
finely grated zest of 1 lime and juice of
   ½ lime
½ tsp sea salt

Heat a large saucepan over medium heat. Add the oil and cook the onions, celery and garlic over low heat for about 10 minutes until softened. Increase the heat, stir in the mince and fry until it has browned, breaking up any large chunks with a wooden spoon.

Add the red wine and stir with a wooden spoon to deglaze, loosening and incorporating any sediment from the bottom of the pan. Bring to the boil and allow to reduce by half.

Stir in the beans, tomatoes and juice from the tin, chilli, cumin, stock, bay leaves, thyme and rosemary. Season with the sea salt and a few twists of black pepper. Bring to a simmer, cover with a lid and cook for at least 1 hour. (If you are using dried kidney beans, you will need to simmer for up to 2 hours, topping up with extra water as needed.) Stir occasionally to prevent sticking, and add a cup of water if it is getting too thick.

While the chilli is cooking, make the smoked paprika butter. Beat together the butter, smoked paprika, lime zest and juice and salt.

Remove the thyme and rosemary sprigs from the chilli and discard. Stir through the coriander and the flavoured butter, then allow to sit for 5 minutes. Add a little more seasoning, if you like, and serve with coriander sprigs scattered over and lime wedges.

Miso-baked cod with sesame dressing and pak choi

This is such a simple dish to prepare, so it's ideal for midweek dinners when you require food fast. The dressing is a fusion of flavours that work really well with the cod; however, other fish can be used here if you prefer. Steamed rice is a good accompaniment, though I'll often roast small florets of cauliflower in a little oil, then toss them in lemon juice and chopped coriander and serve them alongside too.

Serves: 4
Preparation time: 25 minutes
Cooking time: 10 minutes

4 thick cod fillets, skinned
2 tbsp white miso paste
300g pak choi
2 tsp toasted sesame seeds
sea salt

FOR THE DRESSING
50g tahini
1½ tbsp white miso paste
1 tbsp olive oil
1 tbsp rice vinegar
1 tsp agave syrup or honey

Preheat the oven to 220°C/200°C fan/gas 7 and place a baking sheet in the oven to heat up.

Rub the cod fillets with some salt and set aside for 10 minutes. Once the time is up, rinse the cod fillets and pat dry with kitchen paper.

Sit each piece of cod on a large piece of foil. Spread or brush the miso paste over each fillet and pull up the foil edges to seal, leaving plenty of space around the fish so it can steam. Transfer all four parcels to the preheated baking tray and cook for 10 minutes.

Remove from the oven and leave to rest for 5 minutes.

Meanwhile, trim the ends from the pak choi and slice each one in half lengthways. Sit in a steamer set above a pan of boiling water. Steam for 2–3 minutes, until just tender.

To make the dressing, whisk all the ingredients together with 1½ tablespoons of water.

Scatter the toasted sesame seeds over the cod fillets and serve with the sesame dressing and steamed pak choi.

Roast gremolata salmon with polenta chips

Salmon has a richness that can stand up to any strong flavours added to it. This makes it an ideal fish to top with this tangy, herby gremolata. I can't recommend the polenta chips highly enough – in fact, they should come with a warning as they are pretty addictive. *(See images on following pages.)*

Serves: 4
Preparation time: 45 minutes
Cooking time: 25–30 minutes

½ bunch of flat-leaf parsley, leaves
  picked
½ bunch of tarragon, leaves picked
1 tbsp capers
finely grated zest of 1 lemon
2 garlic cloves, chopped
2 tbsp panko breadcrumbs
2 tbsp extra virgin olive oil
4 salmon fillets, skinned
sea salt and freshly ground black pepper

FOR THE POLENTA CHIPS
100g quick-cook polenta
400ml hot Vegetable Stock (page 271)
50g Parmesan cheese, grated
40g butter
vegetable oil, for frying
flour, for dusting

To make the polenta chips, put the polenta in a non-stick pan and gradually pour in the hot stock, whisking all the time to prevent any lumps. Place over medium heat and slowly bring to the boil, whisking frequently and cooking for about 5 minutes.

Remove from the heat, stir in the Parmesan and butter and season with salt and pepper. Line a 20cm square baking tray with clingfilm and pour in the polenta. Using a wet spatula, smooth the surface and even out to about 2.5cm deep. Cover with clingfilm and cool to room temperature, then chill in the fridge for at least 30 minutes (ideally for a couple of hours).

Preheat the oven to 200°C/180°C fan/gas 6.

Pour enough oil into a medium-large saucepan to come up to approximately 3cm and place over high heat. When the polenta is firm, turn out of the tray and cut to chip shapes. Toss in the flour until evenly coated, and shake off any excess. Carefully place in the hot oil, cooking in batches to avoid overcrowding the pan. Fry for 3 minutes until golden brown, remove with a slotted spoon and drain on kitchen paper. Sprinkle with salt.

While the polenta chips are cooking, make the gremolata for the salmon by coarsely chopping the parsley, tarragon and capers together on a chopping board. Put in a bowl and mix in the lemon zest, garlic, breadcrumbs and olive oil. Season well and mix together.

Sit the salmon on a lightly oiled baking tray and spoon the gremolata over the top of each one. Roast in the oven for 8–10 minutes until the salmon is just cooked through. Serve straight away with the polenta chips and Garden Vegetable Salad (see opposite).

Garden vegetable salad

I like to try to get a variety of textures into a salad for both flavour and visual appeal, so by all means swap and change ingredients depending on what is fresh at the time. Baby spinach, watercress, fresh peas, chicory or chard are all great alternatives. Whatever you choose, do make sure you dress the salad just before serving – that way you will retain the crunch and colour. Use your hands to lightly toss in the dressing for an even coating and to prevent soft leaves getting bruised.

(See image on following page.)

Serves: 4
Preparation time: 10 minutes
Cooking time: 1–2 minutes

100g kale, tough stems removed
1 tbsp chopped coriander
1 medium-large fennel, finely sliced
100g sugar snap peas, finely sliced
100g rocket
2 tbsp Basic Vinaigrette (page 273)
sea salt and freshly ground black pepper

Bring a large pan of salted water to the boil and blanch the kale for 1–2 minutes. Refresh in ice-cold water and drain well. Finely shred the leaves and put in a large bowl.

Add the coriander, fennel and sugar snaps to the kale along with the rocket, vinaigrette and seasoning. Toss together and serve straight away.

Curry-spiced salmon with seeded pumpkin salad

I can't get enough of this dish – the flavours are really powerful and bold, it just makes you want more. Try to use thick salmon fillets, using the belly part of the fish – which will retain plenty of juiciness when cooked – rather than the tail end.

Serves: 4
Preparation time: 25 minutes
Cooking time: 40 minutes

4 salmon fillets
1 tsp mild curry powder
1 tsp sea salt
3 tbsp olive oil

FOR THE SALAD
1 small pumpkin, diced into 2cm cubes
1 sweet potato, diced into 2cm cubes
2 tbsp vegetable oil
100g pumpkin seeds
50g sunflower seeds
50g sesame seeds
2 tbsp linseeds
1 tbsp soy sauce
½ bunch of flat-leaf parsley, leaves chopped
½ small bunch of tarragon, leaves chopped
sea salt and freshly ground black pepper

FOR THE DRESSING
50ml sesame or pumpkin oil
50ml extra virgin olive oil
50ml white wine vinegar
8cm piece of fresh ginger, peeled and finely chopped

Preheat the oven to 200°C/180°C fan/gas 6.

To make the pumpkin salad, put the pumpkin, sweet potato and vegetable oil in a roasting tray and toss together. Season well and roast in the oven for 25–30 minutes, stirring a couple of times to ensure even cooking, until golden and tender.

Heat a large frying pan over medium heat and add all of the seeds. Shake around in the pan to toast to a golden brown colour. Add the soy sauce and toss until the seeds are coated. Remove and set aside.

To make the dressing, whisk all of the ingredients together until well combined. Set aside.

For the salmon, mix the curry powder and salt together and use to season the salmon all over.

Heat the olive oil in a large frying pan over high heat. When hot, add the salmon and cook for 2–3 minutes each side, depending on the thickness of the salmon, until crisp on the outside and just cooked in the middle. Remove from the heat and allow the fillets to rest for a couple of minutes.

Toss the roasted pumpkin and sweet potato together with the parsley and tarragon and pour over the dressing. Serve straight away with the salmon.

Seared tuna with marinated tomatoes

You'll need to plan ahead for this dish as the tomatoes do need to be marinated for at least 24 hours before you serve them. Once that stage is done, however, the finishing off is pretty quick. Serve as a light meal just as it is, or with pasta, crushed potatoes or chargrilled bread for something more substantial. *(See image on following pages.)*

Serves: 4
Preparation time: 20 minutes, plus
  24 hours or more for marinating
Cooking time: 4–5 minutes

4 tuna steaks
olive oil, for searing
aged balsamic vinegar, to serve
sea salt and freshly ground black pepper

FOR THE TOMATOES
600g cherry vine tomatoes
25g tomato purée
50ml balsamic vinegar
3–4 sprigs of thyme
2 bay leaves
½ garlic bulb
1 tbsp sugar
1 tsp salt
good pinch of saffron
200ml olive oil, plus extra to cover

To prepare the tomatoes, pick them from the vines. Bring a saucepan of water to the boil and add the tomatoes and blanch for 10–30 seconds, until the skins start to split. Remove with a slotted spoon and plunge into ice-cold water. Leave for 5 minutes, then drain. The skins should have pretty much come off on their own, but if not, remove any remaining skin with a small sharp knife. Prick the tomatoes all over with the tip of the knife and sit in a bowl.

Place all of the remaining marinade ingredients in a small saucepan and gently heat. Add the tomatoes and top up with extra olive oil to ensure they are completely immersed. Cover with clingfilm and leave in a warm place for 12 hours, then transfer to the fridge for a further 12 hours.

A few minutes before you plan on cooking the tuna, remove the tomatoes from the fridge and return to room temperature, or gently warm through in a saucepan.

Heat a non-stick frying pan over high heat. Pat the tuna steaks dry with kitchen paper and season one side with salt and pepper. Add just enough oil to cover the base of the frying pan and heat until the oil is shimmering.

Place the tuna seasoned side down in the hot oil and then season the top with salt and pepper. Turn the heat down to medium-high and leave to cook, undisturbed, for 1 minute.

Flip the tuna over with a fish slice and cook for a further 1 minute, undisturbed. Remove from the pan and leave to rest for a couple of minutes.

Cut each steak across the grain into approximately 5mm thick slices and arrange on serving plates. Using a slotted spoon, remove the tomatoes from the marinade and serve next to the tuna. Drizzle over the balsamic vinegar and the marinade mix.

Chargrilled mackerel with sherry, piquillo peppers, cornichons and ricotta

Mackerel is a versatile fish that stands up to the fierce heat of the barbecue or grill. It is in season over the summer months, too, so you can really make the most of it then. I've paired it here with tangy cornichons, sweet peppers and creamy ricotta — it's a winner.

Serves: 4
Preparation time: 25 minutes
Cooking time: 10 minutes

100g ricotta cheese
grated zest of ½ lemon
160g piquillo peppers in oil, finely sliced
40g cornichon, finely chopped
40g capers, finely chopped
6 mint leaves, finely chopped
8 flat-leaf parsley leaves, finely chopped
2 tbsp extra virgin olive oil
2 tbsp dry sherry, plus 5 tsp extra
8 skin-on mackerel fillets
2 tbsp vegetable oil
sea salt and freshly ground black pepper

Mix together the ricotta and lemon zest and season with salt and pepper. Set aside.

Combine the peppers, cornichon, capers, mint, parsley, olive oil and 2 tablespoons of sherry. Season to taste and set aside.

Heat a grill to its highest setting, or heat a barbecue until hot.

Check the mackerel for pin bones and remove any you feel. Score the skin several times with the tip of a sharp knife to prevent curling when cooking.

Brush both sides of the fish with vegetable oil and season with salt. Place under the grill or on a barbecue, cooking the skin side first, and douse with the 5 teaspoons of sherry as it cooks. When the skin is deeply golden and blistered, flip over to cook the flesh side for 1 minute, until just cooked through.

Put the piquillo pepper mixture on a large platter or individual plates and sit the mackerel on top. Dot the lemon ricotta over the mackerel and serve.

Haddock, leek and mustard gratin

Covering the haddock fillets with rock salt for 10 minutes is an essential part of this recipe. The salt not only delicately seasons the fish but also draws out excess moisture; if it were left in, the end result would be a watery gratin.

Serves: 4
Preparation time: 40 minutes
Cooking time: 20 minutes

4 skinless haddock fillets
8 tbsp rock salt
25g butter
4 large leeks, whites only, thinly sliced
1 tsp fresh thyme leaves
150ml Vegetable Stock (page 271)
sea salt and freshly ground black pepper

FOR THE CRUMB
80g panko breadcrumbs
20g grated Parmesan cheese
20g soft butter
1 tsp fresh thyme leaves, plus extra
   to scatter

FOR THE SAUCE
60g butter
60g plain flour
600ml milk
120g mature Cheddar cheese, grated
1 tbsp wholegrain mustard
1 tbsp English mustard
2 tsp Worcestershire sauce

First make the crumb. Mix everything together in a bowl and set aside.

Put the haddock fillets in a shallow bowl, cover with the rock salt and leave for 10 minutes.

Preheat the oven to 110°C/90°C fan/gas ¼.

Meanwhile, to make the sauce, melt the butter in a saucepan and when it's bubbling stir in the flour. Cook for 30 seconds, then gradually whisk in the milk. Bring to a simmer and cook for 2 minutes, then stir through the cheese to melt. Add both mustards, the Worcestershire sauce and season with salt.

Rinse the salt off the haddock and pat dry with kitchen paper. Sit on a lightly greased baking tray and put in the oven for 10 minutes to partially cook.

Once the fish is cool enough to handle, break the fillets into large flakes.

Increase the oven temperature to 220°C/200°C fan/gas 7.

Melt the butter in a wide pan, add the leeks and cook for 5 minutes, until starting to soften. Add the thyme and stock and cook gently for a further 5 minutes. Gently fold through the flaked haddock, taking care not to break up the fish. Season to taste.

Divide the cooked leeks between four individual gratin dishes. Sit the partially cooked fish on top. Spoon over the mustard cheese sauce and generously scatter over the crumbs and a few thyme leaves. Sit on a baking sheet and bake for 10 minutes, until the crumb is golden and the sauce is bubbling around the edges.

Braised cod with herb vinaigrette, toasted broccoli, sprouts and chestnuts

Braising fish is a failsafe way to make sure it doesn't dry out or overcook. Try to get thick fillets for this, as they will not only look better on the plate but will also have a juicier texture and bigger surface area to absorb the flavoursome vinaigrette.

Serves: 4
Preparation time: 20 minutes
Cooking time: 15 minutes

4 tbsp olive oil
4 thick skin-on cod fillets
250ml Chicken or Vegetable Stock (pages 270–1)
1 head of broccoli, broken into florets
12 Brussels sprouts, quartered
2 garlic cloves, crushed
100g fresh or vacuum-packed chestnuts, finely chopped
sea salt and freshly ground black pepper

FOR THE VINAIGRETTE
¼ bunch of tarragon, leaves picked and finely sliced
¼ bunch of parsley, leaves picked and finely sliced
2 tbsp capers, chopped
½ red onion, finely chopped
4 tbsp white wine vinegar
150ml extra virgin olive oil
1 green chilli, deseeded and finely chopped

To make the vinaigrette, mix all the ingredients together and set aside.

Heat 2 tablespoons of the olive oil in a large non-stick frying pan over high heat. Season the cod well with salt and pepper and carefully place in the pan, skin-side down. Cook for a couple of minutes until the base of the cod is nicely browned, then turn over.

Pour in 200ml of stock and cover the pan loosely with foil. Reduce the heat and simmer for a maximum of 5 minutes, until the cod is just cooked through.

Heat the remaining 2 tablespoons of olive oil in a wide frying pan over high heat until almost smoking. Add the broccoli and sprouts and fry until browned.

Pour in the remaining 50ml of stock and add the crushed garlic, then reduce the heat slightly. Cook for a few minutes until the vegetables are just tender, then stir in the chestnuts.

To serve, divide the vegetables between plates and sit the cod on top. Drizzle generously with the herbed vinaigrette and serve straight away.

Winter veggie burger

Just because you don't eat meat or you choose to have a meat-free meal shouldn't mean you have to miss out on the opportunity of indulging in a decent burger. This is full of amazing earthy flavours and the addition of quinoa gives it a good protein content you don't get in many veggie burgers. What I must add is, make sure you serve this in a decent bun. I like to use brioche burger buns, especially when they are toasted lightly to bring out their sweetness. Don't stop there, though. Some smoky Applewood cheese melting over the top of the burger is a must, as is a dollop of onion marmalade or relish and a garlicky aioli or mayo.

Makes: 8
Preparation time: 30 minutes
Cooking time: 20 minutes

100g quinoa
300g celeriac, grated
olive oil, for frying
250g chestnut mushrooms, cut into 1cm dice
2 × 400g tins cannellini or butter beans, drained
10g tarragon leaves, roughly chopped
10g thyme leaves
200g mozzarella cheese, grated
125g dried panko breadcrumbs
sea salt and freshly ground black pepper

TO SERVE
8 brioche burger buns, cut in half
Applewood cheese, sliced
Onion Marmalade (page 275) or tomato ketchup
Roast Garlic Aioli (page 272) or garlic mayonnaise

Put the quinoa and 200ml of water in a saucepan and bring to the boil over high heat, then boil for 1 minute. Reduce the heat to low, cover and leave to cook for 12 minutes. Remove from the heat and allow to sit for 5 minutes with the lid on. Fork through the quinoa to separate the grains and leave to cool.

Arrange the celeriac in a steamer set above a pan of simmering water and steam for 3 minutes. Transfer to a plate lined with kitchen paper to absorb any excess moisture and leave to cool.

Heat the olive oil in a frying pan and cook the mushrooms until golden and any moisture has evaporated. Leave to cool.

Transfer the cooled quinoa, celeriac and mushrooms to a food processor and add the beans, tarragon, thyme and mozzarella. Pulse-blend until the mixture comes together. Season well and fry a little of the mixture in oil to check for seasoning. Divide the mixture into 8 patties and lightly coat in breadcrumbs. Chill in the fridge for at least 30 minutes to firm up.

Pour olive oil to come 1cm up the side of a frying pan and place over medium heat. Fry the patties (you may need to do this in batches) until golden on each side and heated through.

Heat a grill to medium-high. Lightly toast the cut sides of the brioche buns. Top the burgers with cheese and grill to melt.

To assemble the burger, spread some Onion Marmalade on the bottom halves of the buns and sit the burgers on top. Add a spoon of Roast Garlic Aioli and top with the bun lid.

Truffled mushroom mac 'n' cheese

Who doesn't love a decent bowlful of macaroni cheese? It is the ultimate comfort food and wonderfully simple to make. However, to take this one step further I like to stir through some mushroom purée flavoured with truffle oil before topping with a herby breadcrumb and baking until golden.

Serves: 4
Preparation time: 20 minutes
Cooking time: 40 minutes

325g dried macaroni pasta
100g panko breadcrumbs
2 tsp picked fresh thyme leaves
3 tbsp truffle oil
sea salt and freshly ground black pepper

FOR THE MUSHROOM PURÉE
25g butter
1 shallot, finely chopped
200g mushrooms, chopped
2 garlic cloves, crushed
2 sprigs of thyme
50ml Madeira wine
150ml milk
1 tbsp truffle oil

FOR THE CHEESE SAUCE
75g butter
75g plain flour
650ml milk
100g mature Cheddar cheese, grated
1 tsp Dijon mustard
1 tsp Worcestershire sauce

To make the mushroom purée, melt the butter in a frying pan and sauté the shallot until soft but not coloured.

Add the mushrooms, garlic and thyme. Cook over medium-high heat until the moisture has cooked out of the mushrooms.

Add the Madeira and boil until it has reduced away. Pour in the milk, bring to a simmer, season with salt and pepper, and remove the thyme sprigs. Transfer to a blender or food processor and blitz to a smooth purée. Stir in the truffle oil, check for seasoning and set aside.

To make the cheese sauce, melt the butter in a medium non-stick saucepan until foaming. Add the flour and cook out for about 30 seconds to 1 minute. Gradually whisk in the milk with a balloon whisk and bring to a simmer. Cook for about 2 minutes, until thickened. Stir in the cheese, mustard, Worcestershire sauce and season with salt and pepper.

Preheat the oven to 220°C/200°C fan/gas 7.

Cook the macaroni according to the packet instructions. Drain and mix with the cheese sauce until the pasta is thoroughly coated. Fold through the mushroom purée and spoon into individual dishes or one large dish to share.

Mix together the breadcrumbs, thyme leaves and truffle oil. Scatter over the top of the macaroni and bake in the oven for 20 minutes until bubbling and golden on top.

Courgette and ricotta fritters

These little fritters have been served many times at my home with a drink or two while we catch up on the family's or friends' weekly news. They also work very well served with a mixed green or Garden Vegetable Salad (see page 55) for a light lunch or supper.

To get ahead of time, you can fully prepare these up until the stage of frying and keep uncovered in the fridge for a couple of hours.

Serves: 4
Preparation time: 30 minutes, plus
   30 minutes salting
Cooking time: 15 minutes

1kg courgettes, grated
2 tsp sea salt
2 shallots, roughly chopped
1 garlic clove, crushed
250ml white wine
250g ricotta cheese
grated zest of ½ lemon, plus juice for
   squeezing over
30g panko breadcrumbs, plus 150g for
   coating
vegetable oil, for deep-frying
sea salt and freshly ground black pepper

Put the grated courgette in a colander and sprinkle with the 2 teaspoons of salt. Set over a bowl and leave for 30 minutes to drain.

Put the shallots, garlic and white wine in a saucepan over high heat and bring to the boil. Simmer to reduce in quantity until you have about 3 tablespoons of liquid remaining. Strain through a sieve and discard the shallots and garlic.

Put the courgettes in a clean tea towel and squeeze out as much of the liquid as possible. Tip into a large bowl and add the white wine reduction, ricotta cheese, lemon zest and 30g of breadcrumbs. Season with salt and pepper.

Roll the mixture into balls approximately the size of golf balls, lightly flatten, then roll around in the 150g of breadcrumbs to evenly coat.

Pour enough oil into a wok, large saucepan or deep-fat fryer to come halfway up the pan. Place over medium heat. If using a deep-fat fryer or if you have a thermometer, heat the oil to 180°C. If not, to check the oil is at the right temperature, drop a 2–3cm cube of bread into the hot oil – it should turn golden and crisp in 1 minute.

Fry the fritters in batches for about 3 minutes, until they are golden and crisp. Drain on kitchen paper to absorb excess oil.

Sprinkle the crunchy fritters with sea salt and serve hot with a squeeze of lemon.

Warm chocolate and raspberry pots

This delicious dessert consists of three layers – a tart raspberry layer, a soft chocolate custardy centre and a crunchy chocolate crumble – and it is guaranteed to be a hit with whoever you serve it to. These little pots are even suitable for those who eat a gluten-free diet. For ultimate indulgence, serve with thick cream, crème fraîche or ice-cream.

Serves: 4
Preparation time: 30 minutes
Cooking time: 25 minutes

FOR THE RASPBERRY LAYER
200g fresh or frozen raspberries
50g icing sugar

FOR THE CHOCOLATE LAYER
100ml whipping cream
2 egg yolks
25g caster sugar
190g dark chocolate (preferably 60% cocoa solids), finely chopped

FOR THE CRUMBLE
60g coconut flour
50g demerara sugar
20g cocoa powder
50g soft butter

To make the raspberry layer, place the raspberries and icing sugar in a saucepan and bring to a simmer. Cook for 10 minutes. Pass through a sieve to remove the seeds and divide between four ramekin dishes.

For the chocolate layer, put the cream in a small saucepan and gently bring to the boil. Meanwhile, in a separate heatproof bowl, whisk together the egg yolks and sugar until light and slightly creamy. Pour over the hot cream, whisking to make a smooth, pale yellow mixture.

Return to the pan, use a spatula to stir the mixture continuously over medium-low heat, until it is just thick enough to coat the back of the spatula.

Put the chopped chocolate in a bowl and pour the custard over. Leave for a few minutes to allow the chocolate to melt, then blend with a stick blender until smooth. Pour into the ramekins on top of the raspberry sauce. Cool and store in the fridge.

To make the crumble, preheat the oven to 200°C/180°C fan/gas 6 and line a baking sheet with baking parchment. Put the flour, sugar and cocoa powder in a bowl and add the butter. Use your fingertips to rub the butter into the dry ingredients until you have a breadcrumb-like texture. Tip onto the lined baking sheet. Bake for 8–10 minutes, until lightly crisp.

Top the chocolate pots generously with the crumble, then return to the oven for 5 minutes. Remove and allow the pots to rest for a further 5 minutes before serving with dollops of crème fraîche or ice cream.

Virtuous brownies

As far as a chocolate brownie goes, this one is pretty good for you. It was created at the restaurant as a gluten-free, dairy-free option and has been such a hit in our house that I just had to share it with you. It's sticky and rich, so a little goes a long way, which should mean it will last you some time...I doubt that will be the case, though!

Makes: 20
Preparation time: 20 minutes
Cooking time: 10–15 minutes

110ml aquafaba (the liquid inside a tin of chickpeas)
100g caster sugar
150g dark chocolate (minimum 66% cocoa solids), chopped, plus 50g finely chopped
50g tahini
50g pomace oil
50g dark brown sugar
100g rice milk
150g coconut flour
50g cocoa powder, sifted
1 tsp bicarbonate of soda

Preheat the oven to 170°C/150°C fan/gas 4. Grease and line a 20 × 30cm baking tin with baking parchment.

Whisk the aquafaba until it almost splits. Add the sugar and whisk until glossy.

In a saucepan, melt 150g of the chocolate with the tahini, pomace oil, dark brown sugar and rice milk.

Mix the coconut flour, cocoa and bicarbonate of soda together in a bowl. Tip this into the chocolate–tahini mixture, then fold gently. Add the aquafaba with the 50g chopped chocolate and fold through to combine. Transfer to the prepared tin. Level the surface with a palette knife.

Bake for 10–15 minutes, until set yet slightly soft. Allow to cool completely before cutting into squares.

Forest fruit sorbet

I like the simplicity of this sorbet. It can be made all year round using fresh berries in the summer months or the convenient bags of frozen berries from the supermarket when fresh are out of season.

The addition of rosemary to the sugar syrup brings a delicate aromatic flavour to the sorbet, which I really like. You could swap this herb for lavender or lemon thyme, if you like.

Makes: approx. 750ml
Preparation time: 5 minutes, plus
   freezing time
Cooking time: 5 minutes

150g caster sugar
4 sprigs of rosemary
450g fresh or frozen fruits of the
   forest (cherries, blackberries and
   blackcurrants), defrosted if frozen

TO SERVE
Meringue (page 277)

Put the sugar, rosemary and 150ml of water in a medium saucepan and place over medium heat. Stir until the sugar has melted, then bring to the boil. Cook for 2 minutes, then add the fruit. Return to the boil, reduce the heat and simmer for 3 minutes.

Remove the rosemary sprigs and transfer the fruit mixture to a food processor. Blend until you have a smooth purée.

Strain through a sieve, using the underside of a ladle to press the liquid through. Leave to cool.

Pour the mixture into a metal or plastic freezerproof container. Cover and freeze for about 1½ hours, until the base and sides are starting to freeze. Remove from the freezer and vigorously stir with a balloon whisk (or an electric whisk) until smooth. Refreeze, and then repeat three or four more times at hourly intervals so that you end up with a smooth sorbet. If you have an ice cream machine, follow the manufacturer's instructions and you should have softly frozen sorbet within about 20 minutes.

Serve on its own or with crushed Meringue (page 277).

Burnt honey ice cream and crunchy praline

There is something special about making your own ice cream and it doesn't have to be complicated. Work out what flavour combinations you like and play around, adding them to a basic custard base.

'Burning' the honey adds a lovely richness and takes away the sweetness, creating an interesting aromatic flavour. *(See image on following page.)*

Makes: approx. 750ml
Preparation time: 25 minutes, plus
 chilling and freezing
Cooking time: 15 minutes

50g blossom honey
250ml milk
250ml double cream
6 egg yolks
50g caster sugar

FOR THE PRALINE
40g caster sugar
20g unsalted butter
½ tsp sea salt
40g roasted hazelnuts

Put the honey in a medium-large saucepan over high heat and allow to boil until it becomes a deep golden colour, almost burnt in appearance.

Gradually add the milk and cream and bring to the boil, stirring frequently.

In a mixing bowl, whisk the egg yolks and caster sugar together until well combined. Slowly pour in the hot milk mixture, whisking as you do so.

Return the mixture back into the pan and cook over a very low heat, stirring continuously until the mixture coats the back of a wooden spoon.

Strain through a sieve and allow to cool. Chill in the fridge.

Pour the mixture into a metal or plastic freezerproof container. Cover and freeze for about 1½ hours, until the base and sides are starting to freeze. Remove from the freezer and vigorously stir with a balloon whisk (or an electric whisk) until smooth. Refreeze, and then repeat three or four more times at hourly intervals so that you end up with a smooth, creamy ice cream. If you have an ice cream machine, follow the manufacturer's instructions and you should have softly frozen ice cream within about 20 minutes.

To make the crunchy praline, put the sugar in a small heavy-based saucepan or frying pan. Place over medium heat and leave the sugar to melt and caramelise to a deep golden colour, swirling the pan occasionally to get even caramelisation. Add the butter, salt and nuts, coat well and transfer to a sheet of baking parchment to cool. Once cold, crush with a rolling pin, or briefly whizz in a food processor and set aside.

Serve the ice cream with a little crunchy praline.

Lemon and basil ice cream

The combination of lemon and basil makes a tangy, refreshing flavour, so this is a favourite in the summer just as it is, in a cone or to accompany a crunchy Meringue (see page 277) and some fresh juicy strawberries. *(See image on following page.)*

Makes: approx. 750ml
Preparation time: 15 minutes, plus
    chilling and freezing
Cooking time: 10 minutes

25g bunch of basil
250ml milk
250ml double cream
6 egg yolks
50g caster sugar
50ml Stock Syrup (page 277)
juice of 1 large lemon

Pick the leaves from the basil stalks and set the leaves aside. Put the stalks in a saucepan with the milk and cream. Bring to the boil, stirring frequently.

In a mixing bowl, whisk the egg yolks and caster sugar together until well combined. Strain the hot milk and cream and discard the stalks. Slowly pour the hot milk mixture into the egg yolks, whisking as you do so.

Return the mixture to the pan and cook over a very low heat, stirring continuously until the mixture coats the back of a wooden spoon. Remove from the heat and allow to cool. Chill in the fridge.

Put the reserved basil leaves in a blender with the stock syrup and lemon juice. Blitz to a loose purée.

When the mixture is cold, mix in the basil purée. Leave to infuse for at least 20 minutes. Strain through a fine sieve into a metal or plastic freezerproof container. Cover and freeze for about 1½ hours, until the base and sides are starting to freeze. Remove from the freezer and vigorously stir with a balloon whisk (or an electric whisk) until smooth. Refreeze, and then repeat three or four more times at hourly intervals so that you end up with a smooth, creamy ice cream. If you have an ice cream machine, follow the manufacturer's instructions and you should have softly frozen ice cream within about 20 minutes.

Banoffee bowl

There is a bit of planning ahead required for this one – in making the biscuits and marinating the bananas – but all the elements are super easy and once done the assembly the next day is very quick. If pressed for time, you can use crushed digestive biscuits, but I do recommend you stick with marinating the bananas as it takes them to another level for this very delicious dessert.

Serves: 4
Preparation time: 30 minutes, plus
  overnight marinating
Cooking time: 25 minutes

FOR THE BANANAS
2 large ripe bananas
25ml rum
25ml maple syrup

FOR THE BISCUIT CRUMBS
50g soft butter
75g caster sugar
75g strong bread flour, plus extra for
  dusting
¼ tsp baking powder
pinch of salt
2 tbsp double cream

FOR THE CARAMEL CREAM
100ml whipping cream
juice of ½ lime
pinch of sea salt
200g caramel condensed milk or dulce
  de leche

TO SERVE
100ml double cream, lightly whipped
freshly grated nutmeg

To prepare the bananas, peel and dice them and place in a bowl with the rum and maple syrup. Cover and put in the fridge overnight to marinate.

To make the biscuit crumbs, beat together the butter and sugar until creamy, then fold in the flour, baking powder and salt. Mix in the cream to form a soft dough. Wrap in clingfilm and chill for about 30 minutes.

Preheat the oven to 190°C/170°C fan/gas 5 and line a baking sheet with baking parchment. Roll out the biscuit dough on a lightly floured surface and to approximately 2cm thick. (The shape doesn't matter as it gets broken into crumbs once cooked.) Transfer to the prepared baking sheet and bake for about 25 minutes, until lightly golden and firm.

Once cooked, leave to cool for about 10 minutes, then break into small chunks while still warm.

To make the caramel cream, whisk the cream until it forms firm peaks. Stir the lime juice and salt into the caramel until smooth, then fold in the cream. The caramel cream can be made ahead; simply chill in the fridge in a bowl or piping bag until ready to use.

To assemble the dessert, divide the biscuit chunks into bowls, reserving a few to decorate, and top with the marinated bananas and any syrup they have created. Pipe or spoon the caramel cream on top. Add a dollop of whipped double cream to each bowl and finish with freshly grated nutmeg and some of the biscuit crumbs.

WEEKEND

Banana pain perdu with crispy bacon

This is a deliciously indulgent brunch dish that really must be tried. The sweet and salty combination of caramelised banana and crisp bacon is balanced beautifully with the creamy, soft, eggy bread.

Serves: 4
Preparation time: 15 minutes
Cooking time: 15 minutes

200g caster sugar
3 overripe bananas, roughly chopped
5 eggs, beaten
225ml milk
20ml dark rum
8 thick slices of brioche
8 slices of bacon
25g butter
1 tbsp vegetable oil
maple syrup, for drizzling

Heat a medium saucepan over high heat and add 100g sugar. Allow the sugar to caramelise to a deep golden brown, swirling the pan a little to ensure even cooking. Add the bananas and stir over low heat, until you have a thick paste. Set aside.

Put the eggs, milk, rum and remaining 100g sugar in a baking dish big enough to sit four slices of brioche. Stir well, until the sugar has dissolved.

Spread the caramelised banana paste onto four brioche slices. Sit the four sandwiches in the baking dish and spoon the egg mixture over the top. Leave for about 10 minutes on each side for the egg to completely soak into the brioche.

Heat a grill to high and cook the bacon until golden and crisp. Keep warm.

Melt the butter in a large frying pan over medium heat and add the oil. Add the brioche sandwiches, fry for 2–4 minutes on each side until golden and the egg has just cooked through.

Serve the caramelised banana pain perdu topped with crispy bacon and drizzled with maple syrup.

Scrambled eggs and avocado on toast with chorizo jam

When it gets to the weekend there is nothing better than having a good breakfast that you can take your time over with a pot of coffee and the newspapers. For this recipe the chorizo jam needs advance preparation, but it lasts well in the fridge and can be frozen, so it's a handy go-to for every weekend.

Serves: 2
Preparation time: 15 minutes
Cooking time: 5 minutes

150g Chorizo Jam (page 274)
1 ripe avocado
juice of ½ small lemon
1 tbsp extra virgin olive oil, plus extra for drizzling
4 eggs
50ml single cream or milk
20g butter
2–4 slices of sourdough bread, lightly toasted
sea salt and freshly ground black pepper

Gently warm the chorizo jam in a small pan.

Peel and remove the stone from the avocado, mash the flesh and put in a bowl. Season with salt and pepper and mix with the lemon juice and olive oil.

In a separate bowl, lightly beat the eggs and cream and season with a little salt. Melt the butter in a non-stick saucepan and when it's foaming, pour in the eggs. Use a rubber spatula to gently and slowly stir the eggs until they are soft, creamy and lightly set.

Arrange the toast between serving plates and spread with the chorizo jam. Top with the scrambled eggs. Serve with extra buttered toast, the avocado and a twist of black pepper.

Bacon and egg brioche buns

This is a perfect solution if you have a large crowd to cook breakfast or brunch for, as it's far less taxing than doing a full fry-up. The bacon jam will need to be made ahead and just warmed through before spooning onto the lightly toasted brioche. The grilled bacon and fried egg make a perfect combination, but you could add a field mushroom, too.

Serves: 2
Preparation time: 5 minutes
Cooking time: 10 minutes

6 slices of smoked streaky bacon
100g Bacon Jam (page 274)
2 brioche burger buns
butter, for frying
2 eggs
sea salt and freshly ground black pepper

Preheat the grill. Arrange the bacon on a tray and grill until golden.

Gently warm the bacon jam in a small pan.

Slice the brioche buns in half and lightly toast the cut sides under the grill.

Meanwhile, melt the butter in a medium non-stick frying pan until frothy and then gently break the eggs into the pan. Fry for 2–3 minutes until the whites are set and season with a little salt and pepper.

Spoon the warmed bacon jam onto the bottom halves of the brioche. Lay the bacon on top of the jam, followed by the fried egg. Top with the other brioche half and serve straight away.

Pan-fried mushrooms with baked eggs and tarragon

You can enjoy this any time of the day, from breakfast right through to late at night. Use any mushrooms you wish — a selection is great — and serve with some good crusty bread to wipe up the juices.

Serves: 2
Preparation time: 5 minutes
Cooking time: 10–15 minutes

1 tbsp vegetable oil
300g mushrooms, cut to similar sizes
15g butter
1 sprig of tarragon, leaves chopped, plus
    extra to serve
splash of sherry vinegar
1 tbsp cream cheese or mascarpone
4 eggs
sea salt and freshly ground black pepper

Preheat the grill to medium-high.

Put a medium-large frying pan over high heat. Add the oil and when hot fry the mushrooms until they are golden. Season with salt and black pepper.

Add the butter and toss the mushrooms around in the pan for a few moments, then stir through the tarragon, vinegar and cheese. Cook for a couple of minutes, then crack the eggs on top of the mushrooms, season again and place under the grill. Cook for 3–4 minutes or until the eggs are cooked to your liking. Serve straight away with the extra tarragon sprinkled over.

Sweetcorn and tarragon fritters

Savoury pancakes or fritters are usually a popular choice in my household when we are having a late breakfast. We'll often top these with a spoonful of crème fraîche and some crispy bacon or chorizo. You could even add a spoon of the Bacon Jam or Chorizo Jam from page 274 if you so wish.

I like to use fresh corn on the cob for these when in season, as it gives a better crunch. If you don't want to use tarragon, then chives, basil or parsley work well too.

Makes: 10
Preparation time: 10 minutes
Cooking time: 10 minutes

2 corn on the cobs, husks removed, or
    150g frozen sweetcorn
150g plain flour
1 tsp baking powder
1 egg
125ml whole milk
1 tbsp chopped tarragon leaves
groundnut or vegetable oil, for frying

Bring a pan of salted water to the boil and cook the corn on the cob for 8 minutes. Drain, allow to cool enough to handle, then cut off the kernels. Alternatively, if you are using frozen sweetcorn, cook for 4–5 minutes, then drain.

Sift the flour and baking powder into a bowl.

In another bowl, beat together the egg and milk, then pour into the flour. Mix until smooth, then season and mix in the corn and tarragon, being careful not to overmix as the fritters won't be fluffy.

Heat a large frying pan over medium heat. Add enough oil to cover the base of the pan and, when hot, drop spoonfuls of the batter in the pan. Cook the fritters for a couple of minutes, until small bubbles appear on the surface and the edges are drying out. Use a fish slice to flip the fritter over and fry the other side for a minute or so, until golden. Continue with the remaining mixture and serve the fritters hot.

Hazelnut and fennel granola

This is a really crunchy granola with a bold flavour that works well served with thick Greek yoghurt and some diced pear or banana. However, the combination of fennel seeds and hazelnuts makes this really versatile, so it can also be used to scatter over salads such as roasted carrot and beetroot, or over vegetable gratins as an alternative to breadcrumbs.

Serves: 8–10
Preparation time: 5 minutes
Cooking time: 20–25 minutes

350g blanched hazelnuts
15g fennel seeds
200g jumbo oats
125g caster sugar
125g golden syrup

Preheat the oven to 200°C/180°C fan/gas 6.

Put the hazelnuts on a baking tray and toast for 5 minutes, add the fennel seeds and cook for a further 5 minutes. Cool slightly, then lightly crush. Transfer to a mixing bowl and add the oats.

Put the sugar in a saucepan and add 3 tablespoons of water. Bring to the boil over high heat and cook for 3 minutes until it is syrupy but not yet caramelising.

Add the golden syrup to the sugar syrup, then pour over the nuts, oats and fennel seeds. Mix well, then spread onto a baking sheet lined with baking parchment. Bake in the oven for 10 minutes, stirring a couple of times to ensure even toasting, until golden and caramelised.

Remove from the oven, leave to cool completely, then store in an airtight container.

Gluten-free granola

The idea for this recipe came from one of the restaurants where we have many requests for gluten-free options. I like to make this at home for us to have as a healthy breakfast, too, served with milk or yoghurt and topped with some fresh berries or banana.

Serves: 8–10
Preparation time: 5 minutes
Cooking time: 20 minutes

200g gluten-free oats
10g quinoa flakes
50g sesame seeds
50g sunflower seeds
70g pumpkin seeds
6 tbsp coconut oil, melted
50g agave syrup
100g dates, finely chopped

Preheat the oven to 200°C/180°C fan/gas 6.

Put the oats, quinoa and all of the seeds in a roasting tray and mix in the coconut oil.

Place in the oven and bake for 15 minutes until golden, turning in the tray a couple of times to ensure even toasting.

Pour over the agave syrup, add the dates and mix to combine, then return to the oven for a further 5 minutes.

Remove from the oven, leave to cool completely and store in an airtight container.

Spicy chilli-glazed chicken wings

There are three stages to this, which gives you an utterly delicious end result, so don't, I repeat, don't, be tempted to skip anything. The chicken wings need to be left in brine for 24 hours, so make sure you factor in this time if you're going to make this – or should I say, 'when you make it'?

Serves: 4
Preparation time: 25 minutes, plus 1 hour cooling and 24 hours brining
Cooking time: 1 hour 45 minutes– 1 hour 50 minutes

1kg chicken wings (preferably corn-fed)

FOR THE BRINE
175g sea salt
1 tbsp white peppercorns
1 tbsp coriander seeds
1 tbsp fennel seeds
3 bay leaves
few sprigs of thyme

FOR THE DRY RUB
25g dark brown sugar
25g caster sugar
2 tsp smoked paprika
1 tbsp paprika
2 tsp garlic salt
1 tsp sea salt

FOR THE GLAZE
45g apricot jam
1 tbsp light soy sauce
1 tbsp sriracha sauce (hot chilli sauce)
2 tsp white wine vinegar

To make the brine, put all of the ingredients in a large saucepan, add 2.5 litres of cold water and bring to the boil. Remove from the heat and leave to cool. When cold, add the chicken wings and leave them in the brine for 24 hours.

The next day, make the dry rub by simply mixing everything together in a bowl, then set aside.

Preheat the oven to 140°C/120°C fan/gas 1.

Remove the wings from the brine, rinse under cold water and pat dry with kitchen paper. Toss the wings in the dry rub and arrange them in a single layer on a baking tray. Bake for 1½ hours, increase the heat to 220°C/200°C fan/gas 7, then continue to cook for a further 15–20 minutes, until golden and sticky.

Meanwhile, make the glaze. Combine the ingredients in a saucepan and heat until warmed. When the chicken wings are ready, brush the sticky glaze all over while hot and serve straight away.

Sunday roast chicken

When it comes to making a Sunday roast for all the family, I quite like to throw a load of veg into the roasting tray alongside the chicken to serve as an accompaniment. They provide additional flavour to the meat and cooked this way means it saves on the washing up! In addition these roasted veg create a flavoursome base to make a gravy or sauce. I must add, though, that to ensure you end up with a really delicious result, you should buy the best free-range or organic chicken you can, no matter how many veg you put in the tray. *(See image on following pages.)*

Serves: 6
Preparation time: 20 minutes
Cooking time: 1 hour 25 minutes

1 large chicken
50g soft butter
2 garlic cloves, crushed
¼ bunch of thyme, leaves picked
½ tsp English mustard powder
½ tsp sea salt
½ tsp freshly ground black pepper
olive oil, for drizzling
4 small-medium onions, cut into wedges
¼ bunch of thyme
2 bay leaves
1 garlic bulb, halved horizontally
200ml white wine
350ml Chicken Stock (page 270)
1 tsp Marmite
2 tbsp sweet sherry
2 tsp wholegrain mustard
100ml crème fraîche
sea salt and freshly ground black pepper

Preheat the oven to 190°C/170°C fan/gas 5.

Remove any strings and giblets from the chicken. Mix the butter with the garlic, thyme leaves, mustard powder and ½ teaspoon each of salt and pepper. Use your hands to smear two-thirds of the flavoured butter under the skin of the chicken, all over the flesh of the breasts and legs. With the remaining third, smear the top of the chicken.

Season the inside cavity with salt and pepper. Sit the chicken in a lightly greased roasting tray and scatter around the onions, thyme sprigs, bay leaves and garlic bulb. Roast in the oven for 20–25 minutes until the chicken starts to take on a golden colour. Pour the wine over the top of the vegetables and cover the whole tray loosely with foil, allowing some steam to escape.

Continue to roast for a further 50 minutes to 1 hour, until the chicken is cooked through. To check, insert a skewer into the thickest part of the thigh – if the juices run clear it is ready. If not, continue to cook for a further 10 minutes and test again. Remove the chicken from the tray to a large dish. Loosely cover with the foil and leave to rest for 10–15 minutes.

Put the roasting tray directly on the hob over medium heat and stir in the stock, Marmite and sherry, scraping the bottom of the pan to maximise flavour. Bring to the boil and simmer for 10 minutes.

Remove the garlic, thyme and bay leaves. Scrape everything into a large bowl and, using a stick blender, pulse in the mustard and crème fraîche. Keep pulsing until the gravy takes on a saucy consistency. Add a little more seasoning, if you like, and transfer to a jug. Carve the chicken and serve with the gravy.

Pancetta-wrapped sprouts

Serves: 6
Preparation time: 25 minutes
Cooking time: 10 minutes

300g Brussels sprouts
150g pancetta slices
2 tbsp vegetable oil

Bring a pan of salted water to the boil. Add the sprouts, return to the boil and cook for 1 minute. Drain and put into ice-cold water for about 5 minutes. Drain and pat dry with a clean tea towel.

Wrap each sprout in the pancetta, trimming the slices if the sprouts are small. Place in the fridge if you are not cooking them straight away.

Heat the oil in a large frying pan over medium-high heat. Fry the sprouts in the oil until heated through and the pancetta is golden. Drain on kitchen paper and serve hot.

Sunday roast potatoes

Serves: 6
Preparation time: 10 minutes, plus
    1 hour drying
Cooking time: 45–50 minutes

1.5kg potatoes (King Edward or Maris
    Piper), peeled and evenly chopped
1 tsp sea salt, plus extra to sprinkle
75g duck fat
75ml vegetable oil
¼ bunch of thyme
3 garlic cloves, peeled and left whole

Put the potatoes in a large saucepan and cover with cold water. Add the salt, bring to the boil, cover, reduce to a simmer and cook for about 15 minutes until just about tender. Drain and shake them in the pan fairly vigorously to rough up the edges. Lay out in a single layer to cool and put in the freezer for 1 hour to dry, or the fridge.

Preheat the oven to 220°C/200°C fan/gas 7. Put the duck fat and vegetable oil in a large deep-sided roasting tray and put into the oven for 10 minutes. Carefully remove from the oven and put the dry potatoes in one by one using tongs.

Season, add the thyme and garlic and baste the potatoes with the oil. Roast in the oven for 30–40 minutes, basting frequently with the hot fat. When the potatoes are golden and crunchy, use a slotted spoon to lift them out of the tray and onto kitchen paper to absorb excess fat. Sprinkle with a little salt and serve.

Roast carrots

Serves: 6
Preparation time: 10 minutes
Cooking time: 20 minutes

30ml olive oil
6 large carrots, halved
25g unsalted butter, diced
4 sprigs of thyme
1 star anise
½ tsp sea salt

Preheat the oven to 220°C/200°C fan/gas 7. Put the oil in a roasting tray and place in the oven to heat up for 5 minutes.

Add the carrots cut-side down to the hot tray. Toss in the remaining ingredients and roast for 20 minutes, until the carrots are golden and soft.

Buttermilk fried chicken

I have to admit, this is a bit of a guilty pleasure in my household. On the occasional Saturday night when we are all home, we like to tuck into these crunchy, tender chicken pieces along with a crisp green salad, grilled corn on the cob and Ranch Dressing (see page 273).

The key for really tender chicken is to allow plenty of time for it to marinate in the buttermilk — as much as 48 hours if you can plan that far ahead.

Serves: 4–6
Preparation time: 15 minutes, plus
   8 hours (or longer) marinating
Cooking time: 20 minutes

1kg boneless, skinless chicken thighs
groundnut oil, for frying
spring onions, sliced, to serve
dried chilli flakes, to serve

FOR THE MARINADE
400ml buttermilk
400ml whole milk
1 shallot, sliced
½ red chilli, sliced
zest of ½ lime, plus extra to serve
1 tsp sea salt

FOR THE CRUMB
150g plain flour
75g porridge oats
2 tsp onion powder
2 tsp garlic powder
1 tsp sea salt
1 tsp smoked paprika
1½ tsp fresh thyme leaves

TO SERVE
Ranch Dressing (page 273)

Mix together all the marinade ingredients in a large bowl. Add the chicken, making sure to completely coat in the buttermilk mix. Cover and refrigerate for 8 hours or up to 48 hours.

Before cooking, return the chicken to room temperature by leaving it out of the fridge for up to 1 hour.

Put the ingredients for the crumb in a shallow bowl and use a balloon whisk to combine well.

Preheat the oven to 180°C/160°C fan/gas 4. Fill a wide straight-sided pan with groundnut oil to come up to about 2cm, and heat until very hot (about 180°C). If you don't have a thermometer, drop a cube of bread in to check the temperature of the oil — it should brown almost immediately.

Shake as much buttermilk marinade off the chicken pieces as possible and toss them in the crumb mixture until thoroughly coated.

Put the chicken pieces in a single layer in the hot oil (in batches depending on the size of your pan) and fry for a couple of minutes, until golden and crisp. Carefully turn the pieces over using tongs and cook for a further 2 minutes.

Remove and drain on kitchen paper, then transfer to a roasting tray. Repeat with the remaining chicken if necessary.

Put the chicken in the oven and bake for up to 15 minutes, until crunchy rather than just crisp. Serve with a sprinkling of spring onions, dried chilli flakes and lime quarters, and Ranch Dressing, if you like.

Chicken, ham and mushroom puff pie

When cooking this at home, for ease and to avoid any pastry wastage, I make a rectangular pie using ready rolled puff pastry from the freezer.

As a family we will often have this on a Sunday as an alternative to a roast. The filling is best spread onto the pastry when chilled, so Saturday afternoon or evening is the ideal time to make it.

Serves: 6–8
Preparation time: 25 minutes plus at
    least 4 hours chilling
Cooking time: 40 minutes

2 × 320g sheets of ready rolled all-butter
    puff pastry
2 egg yolks
½ tsp nigella or black sesame seeds,
    to sprinkle
½ tsp rock salt, to sprinkle

FOR THE FILLING
25g unsalted butter
1 onion, peeled and diced
2 celery sticks, chopped
1 medium-large leek, white part only,
    thinly sliced
100g button mushrooms, halved or
    quartered if large
4 skinless, boneless chicken breasts
    (approx. 500g), cut into 2–3cm chunks
2 tbsp plain flour
4 tbsp dry sherry
juice of ½ lemon
200ml Chicken Stock (page 270)
4 tbsp crème fraîche
1 tbsp Dijon mustard
handful of chopped flat-leaf parsley
handful of chopped tarragon
150g piece cooked ham, cut into 2cm
    chunks
sea salt and freshly ground black pepper

To make the filling, heat a large saucepan over medium heat and melt the butter. Add the onion, celery, leek and mushrooms and gently cook for about 8 minutes until softened but not coloured. Season to taste.

Increase the heat, season the chicken and add to the pan. Fry for a few minutes until the chicken starts to turn golden. Mix in the flour and cook for about 30 seconds, stirring to prevent sticking. Season with flaked sea salt and freshly ground black pepper.

Pour in the sherry, stir with a wooden spoon to deglaze, loosening and incorporating any sediment from the bottom of the pan, then add the lemon juice and stock. Bring to the boil and simmer for 5 minutes, until the sauce thickens and the chicken cooks through. Stir in the crème fraîche, Dijon mustard and herbs. Add a little more seasoning, if you like, and remove from the heat. Leave to cool, then chill in the fridge for a few hours or overnight.

Preheat the oven to 200°C/180°C fan/gas 6, and put a large baking sheet in the oven to heat.

Remove the mixture from the fridge and stir in the ham chunks. Unroll one sheet of pastry and lightly score a 1cm border around the edges using the tip of a sharp knife, taking care not to cut right through. Brush the outer border with some egg yolk.

Spoon the filling into the centre of the pastry and spread to the border. Unroll the second piece of pastry on top and press the edges together using the tip of your knife. Brush the surface with egg yolk, then score a pattern on the surface.

Sprinkle over the seeds and salt and gently slide the pie onto the hot oven sheet. Bake for 30 minutes, until the pastry is golden brown and crisp.

Aromatic poached and barbecued chicken

Poaching a whole chicken before finishing it off on the griddle or barbecue ensures the meat stays juicy and won't dry out from the intense direct heat of the second-stage cooking. The aromatic poaching liquor is then reduced to make a rich glaze, so there's no holding back on flavour here. *(See image on following pages.)*

Serves: 4
Preparation time: 15 minutes
Cooking time: 1 hour 45 minutes

3 tbsp olive oil
1 onion, quartered
2 celery sticks, halved
1 leek, white part only, halved
2 carrots, quartered
1 garlic bulb, halved
2 cinnamon sticks
3 star anise
1 orange, quartered
2 red chillies, halved
¼ bunch of coriander stalks, leaves
  reserved for serving
8cm piece of fresh ginger, peeled and
  roughly chopped
250ml Madeira wine
2 litres Chicken or Vegetable Stock
  (pages 270–1)
1 tbsp soy sauce
4 tbsp hoisin sauce
2 tbsp honey
1 large corn-fed chicken

Heat the oil in a large saucepan over medium heat. Add the onion, celery, leek, carrots, garlic, spices, orange, chillies, coriander stalks and ginger. Cook, stirring occasionally, until the vegetables are browned.

Pour in the Madeira wine and simmer, uncovered, until it is reduced and syrupy in consistency. Add all of the remaining ingredients apart from the chicken and bring back to the simmer.

Add the chicken to the pan, return to the simmer and cover with a lid.

Leave to gently poach over low heat for 1 hour. Turn off the heat and leave the chicken to sit in the cooking liquid for a further 20 minutes.

Carefully remove the chicken from the pan allowing all the liquid to drain from inside the bird. Sit on a tray, cover with clingfilm or foil and set aside.

Preheat your barbecue or a griddle pan.

Strain the cooking liquid into a wide-bottomed pan and then bring to the boil. Reduce by about two-thirds – you should have a gravy-like sauce (this can take quite a while).

Brush the sauce all over the chicken and barbecue or griddle over medium heat until the skin is deeply caramelised all over. Serve any remaining sauce on the side and scatter the coriander leaves over the chicken to finish.

Barbecued vegetable salad

Vegetables cook really well on a barbecue when it is not too hot, especially when they are marinated. If the grill is too hot the garlic, ginger, lemongrass and chilli will burn and therefore taste bitter. If you've not got time to marinate the veg you can simply coat them in oil and drizzle them with lime juice and sesame oil.

(See image on following pages.)

Serves: 4
Preparation time: 20 minutes, plus
  3–24 hours marinating
Cooking time: approx. 10 minutes

8 garlic cloves
1 red chilli, halved and deseeded
1 lemongrass stalk, roughly chopped
2cm piece of fresh ginger, peeled and
  roughly chopped
2 bay leaves
150ml vegetable oil
1 tsp sea salt
1–1.2kg assorted vegetables (such as
  asparagus, baby aubergine, baby
  fennel, courgette, sweet potatoes,
  red, orange or yellow peppers, spring
  onions)
1 tbsp rice vinegar
½ bunch of coriander, leaves picked and
  chopped
50g roasted salted peanuts, roughly
  chopped

Put the garlic, chilli, lemongrass, ginger and bay leaves in a blender or small food processor and blitz together. Blend in the oil and season with 1 teaspoon of sea salt.

To prepare the vegetables, halve the asparagus, baby aubergine, fennel and courgette lengthways, cut the peppers into 2cm strips (removing the seeds), peel and cut the sweet potato into slim wedges and trim the tops and base off the spring onions.

Mix the vegetables with the garlic mixture and leave to marinate for at least 3 hours, but ideally nearer to 24 hours, turning occasionally.

When ready, heat up your barbecue until hot. Arrange the vegetables in a single layer on the wire rack and turn with tongs. Cooking times will vary depending on the thickness of the vegetables, with the sweet potatoes and fennel taking the longest (about 10 minutes) and spring onions being the quickest (about 2 minutes). Keep turning the vegetables and you will feel when they are done.

Arrange the barbecued vegetables on a serving platter and sprinkle over the rice vinegar. Scatter with chopped coriander and roasted peanuts.

Bulgar wheat and barley salad

This is just as good, if not better, eaten the day after making it, as all the flavours blend and the salad becomes even more tasty. It's a versatile salad that's become a regular during the summer months at my house. It can accompany pretty much anything. Brown rice can be used instead of bulgar wheat, if you so wish. *(See image on previous pages.)*

Serves: 4
Preparation time: 20 minutes
Cooking time: 35 minutes

50g pearl barley
50g bulgar wheat
1 large bunch of flat-leaf parsley
1 small bunch of mint
4 tomatoes
1 small red onion, finely chopped
45g semi-dried tomatoes, chopped

FOR THE DRESSING
juice of 2 lemons
4 tbsp extra virgin olive oil
1 tsp mixed allspice
½ tsp smoked paprika
sea salt and freshly ground black pepper

Cook the pearl barley in boiling water for 20 minutes until tender. Drain, refresh under cold water and allow to cool completely.

Meanwhile, rinse the bulgar wheat in a sieve under cold water. Put in a pan, cover with at least three times the amount of water and add a pinch of salt. Throw in the parsley and mint stalks, reserving the leaves. Bring to the boil, cover and simmer for 15 minutes. When cooked, drain well and leave to cool completely.

Put the tomatoes in a bowl and pour over boiling water. Leave for a few seconds until the skins start to blister. Transfer to a bowl of ice-cold water to cool and then remove the skins. Cut the skinned tomatoes into quarters, remove the seeds and cut the flesh into small dice. Put in a large bowl.

Finely chop the parsley and mint leaves together and add to the tomatoes along with the onion and semi-dried tomatoes.

In a separate bowl, make the dressing by mixing together the lemon juice, extra virgin olive oil, allspice, smoked paprika and seasoning.

Add the pearl barley and bulgar wheat to the herb bowl and gently combine. Pour over the dressing and fold together. Serve at room temperature.

Sweetcorn, chorizo and toasted almond salad

This salad certainly doesn't lack in flavour and makes for a great accompaniment to any barbecued dish. The vibrant mix of charred corn, smoky chorizo, fresh herbs, spices and tangy bite from the capers and vinegar creates such a wonderful flavour and I think you'll agree, it looks pretty good too. *(See image on previous pages.)*

Serves: 4
Preparation time: 15 minutes
Cooking time: 15 minutes

8 cobs of corn, husks removed
4 tbsp vegetable oil
2 tsp flaked sea salt
200g chorizo, skin removed and diced
25g butter
100g blanched almonds, roughly
  chopped
½ tsp ground cumin
½ tsp ground coriander
½ bunch of tarragon, leaves chopped
½ bunch of flat-leaf parsley, leaves
  chopped

FOR THE DRESSING
2 tbsp capers, finely chopped
50ml extra virgin olive oil
2 tbsp sherry vinegar
sea salt and freshly ground black pepper

Bring a large pan of salted water to the boil and cook the corn for 5 minutes. Pat dry and brush with the oil. Sprinkle over the salt and cook on a hot barbecue (or chargrill pan) to evenly char until golden brown. Set aside to cool down.

When the corn is cool enough to handle, slice off the kernels into a serving bowl.

Heat a dry non-stick frying pan over medium heat and add the chorizo. Fry for 5–10 minutes until browned all over.

Melt the butter in a frying pan and, when it is foaming, add the almonds. Stir the almonds around in the pan until deep golden. Add the cumin, coriander and a good pinch of salt. Use a slotted spoon to remove the almonds, leaving behind the excess butter. Add the almonds to the corn along with the chorizo, tarragon and parsley.

In a separate bowl, mix together the capers, olive oil and vinegar for the dressing. Season with salt and freshly ground black pepper and drizzle over the salad just before serving.

Spiced honey glazed pork belly

People are often scared of cooking pork because they think it's dry and not very appetising. Cooked the right way, this meat is absolutely delicious. Here the pork belly is slowly cooked in a flavoursome stock, ensuring that it doesn't dry out at all. The sticky aromatic glaze is the ideal finishing touch, and accompanied with sticky rice and steamed greens, you really can't go wrong.

Serves: 8
Preparation time: 15 minutes
Cooking time: 2 hours 20 minutes, plus cooling

1 pork belly, halved widthways
2 tbsp smoked paprika
1 onion, quartered
1 leek, white part only, quartered lengthways
1 garlic bulb, halved
2 celery sticks, quartered
1 bay leaf
small bunch of thyme
pinch of sea salt

FOR THE GLAZE
1 tbsp coriander seeds
3 tsp ground cinnamon
4 star anise
150ml port
150ml honey
150ml rice wine vinegar

Put the pork in a large saucepan with the paprika, onion, leek, garlic, celery, bay leaf, thyme and a good pinch of salt. Pour in enough water to make sure the pork is completely immersed.

Place the pan over high heat and bring to a simmer. Reduce the heat to medium, cover with a lid and cook for 2–3 hours, until a knife slides through.

Remove from the heat and leave the pork to steep in the pan until it is cool enough to handle. Use tongs to remove the pork from the liquid and trim away the fatty skin. Slice the pork into 5cm wide strips.

To make the glaze, lightly crush the coriander seeds in a pestle and mortar and place in a saucepan. Add the remaining ingredients and bring to a simmer. Cook for about 10 minutes, until it reaches a thick sauce consistency.

Heat a frying pan over high heat. Brush the glaze over the pork belly strips and add them to the pan. Pan-fry for 3–5 minutes on each side, until browned. Serve hot.

Pulled pork sliders with apple and ginger

This is a treat for the weekend. The beauty of this recipe is that you can leave the pork belly to gently cook in the liquor for a good few hours while you get on with weekend errands, then simply shred it and assemble the buns with a few accompaniments. The ingredients list may look long, but the preparation and cooking part is exceptionally straightforward. *(See image on previous pages.)*

Makes: 16–20 sliders (or 8 regular burgers)
Preparation time: 20 minutes
Cooking time: 3 hours 30 minutes

2 tbsp vegetable oil
1 small onion, quartered
1 celery stick, halved
½ leek, white part only, halved
1 carrot, quartered
2 garlic cloves, lightly crushed
1 cinnamon stick
2 star anise
1 red chilli, halved
½ orange, halved
½ bunch of coriander
250ml sweet sherry
2 tbsp hoisin sauce
1 tbsp honey
1 litre Chicken Stock (page 270)
1 tbsp soy sauce
2kg boneless pork belly

TO SERVE
16 brioche sliders or 8 brioche burger buns, sliced in half
1–2 Granny Smith apples, sliced thinly
stem ginger in syrup, sliced thinly

Heat the oil in a large saucepan. Add the onion, celery, leek, carrot and garlic and fry until the vegetables start to brown. Add the cinnamon, star anise, chilli, orange, coriander, sherry, hoisin sauce, honey, stock, sauce and pork. Bring to a very gentle simmer, cover and cook over low heat for 3 hours.

Carefully remove the pork using tongs, and set aside to cool slightly. Strain the stock into a clean saucepan and put the pan over high heat. Bring to the boil and cook until sauce-like in consistency and reduced by about half.

Using two forks, gently pull the pork belly apart, discard the skin and place in a bowl. Add a few spoonfuls of the reduced sauce, just enough to bind the pork together. Heat in a pan if it requires it.

Lightly toast the cut sides of the brioche buns under a preheated grill. Top the bases with pulled pork, followed by the apple and ginger. Pop the bun lids on and serve hot.

Homemade pork and oat sausages with sage and onion marmalade

If you've become wary of buying sausages for fear of not knowing what's in them, then you really must give these a go – simple, honest ingredients that are shaped and wrapped in clingfilm before being poached (no messing about with sausage skins). Once cooked, you finish them off in a frying pan for a golden colour, then serve them with a sweet onion marmalade. Oh, and mashed potatoes on the side is a must.

Makes: 12 sausages
Preparation time: 40 minutes
Cooking time: 40 minutes

2 tbsp vegetable oil, plus extra for frying
1 onion, diced
1 garlic clove, crushed
¼ bunch of thyme, leaves only
400g pork mince
200g plain pork sausage meat
100g oats
¼ bunch of sage, leaves finely chopped
¼ bunch of flat-leaf parsley, leaves chopped
½ nutmeg, freshly grated
1 egg
sea salt and freshly ground black pepper

FOR THE MARMALADE
25g butter
3 onions, thinly sliced
1 garlic clove, crushed
75ml balsamic vinegar
2 tbsp soft dark brown sugar
¼ bunch of sage, leaves finely chopped

To make the sausages, heat the oil in a saucepan and gently sauté the onion, garlic and thyme leaves until the onion is softened but not coloured. Transfer to a mixing bowl to cool.

Add the pork mince, sausage meat, oats, sage, parsley, nutmeg and egg to the bowl with the cooled onions, and season with salt and black pepper. Mix until well combined. Fry a little of the sausage mixture in a small frying pan, taste, and add a little more seasoning if you like.

Divide the sausage mixture into six. Lay a large sheet of clingfilm on the worktop. Place one-sixth of the mixture along the edge, then roll the clingfilm over to form a sausage shape. Twist and tie the ends together, and twist in the middle to create two sausages. Repeat with the remaining sausage mixture – you should have 12 sausages in total.

Bring a large saucepan of water to the boil, add the sausages and simmer for 8 minutes. Remove, drain and refrigerate.

To make the marmalade, melt the butter in a large saucepan. Add the onions and garlic, and season well with salt and black pepper. Gently cook for about 20 minutes until the onions are deep golden and caramelised. Increase the heat to high, add the balsamic vinegar, stir with a wooden spoon to deglaze, loosening and incorporating any sediment from the bottom of the pan. Add the brown sugar and sage, then cook for a further 5 minutes. Season to taste. Remove from the heat and allow to cool to room temperature.

Heat a dash of oil in a large frying pan over medium heat. Unwrap the sausages and fry for 8–10 minutes, until golden and cooked through. Serve with the marmalade on the side.

Lamb and saffron tagine

If you want something easy to prepare and serve your friends over the weekend, you can't go wrong with a tagine. The key to getting the most wonderfully flavoured lamb is to marinate it for up to 48 hours before slowly cooking it in the tagine sauce. Serve with couscous mixed with chopped preserved lemon and stir through some fresh mint or coriander leaves.

Serves: 6
Preparation time: 25 minutes plus up to 48 hours marinating
Cooking time: 2½–3 hours

1.8kg diced neck or shoulder of lamb
2 tbsp vegetable oil
2 large onions, chopped
3 garlic cloves, crushed
2cm piece of fresh ginger, peeled and grated
800ml passata or tinned chopped tomatoes
750ml Chicken Stock (page 270)
2 tsp saffron stands, soaked in 1 tbsp warm water
200g dried dates, halved
100g golden sultanas
75g chopped pistachios
sea salt and freshly ground black pepper

FOR THE MARINADE
2 tsp ground black pepper
2 tsp turmeric
2 tsp ground cinnamon
1½ tsp paprika
1 tsp cayenne pepper
2 tbsp groundnut oil

Place the marinade spices in a large bowl and mix to combine. Add the oil and lamb. Mix to coat the lamb. Cover and leave to marinate overnight or for up to 48 hours.

Heat the oven to 150°C/130°C fan/gas 2.

Put a large casserole over medium heat with 1 tablespoon of oil. Sauté the onions for around 10 minutes until they are softened but not coloured. Add the garlic and ginger for the last 3–4 minutes.

While the onions are cooking, heat the remaining 1 tablespoon of oil in a large frying pan and place over high heat. Add the lamb and brown on all sides.

Pour around half of the stock into the lamb to deglaze the pan, and transfer everything to the casserole with the onions.

Add the passata or tomatoes, remaining stock, saffron and soaking liquid, dates, sultanas and most of the pistachios.

Bring to the boil, cover with a lid and transfer to the oven for 2–2½ hours until the meat is tender and the sauce thickened. Serve sprinkled with chopped mint and the remaining pistachios.

Slow-roast leg of lamb and fresh mint sauce

You really shouldn't rush the cooking of a whole leg of lamb, and the secret to getting tender meat that's infused with plenty of flavour is to baste it frequently. This recipe makes its own delicious gravy, too, and it is perfect for a big meal with friends and family. *(See image on following pages.)*

Serves: 6
Preparation time: 15 minutes
Cooking time: 3 hours 45 minutes

2 large onions, quartered
1 leg of lamb, approx. 1.8kg
3 garlic cloves, peeled
2 tbsp chopped rosemary
1 tbsp thyme leaves
grated zest of 1 lemon
2 tsp sweet paprika
1 tbsp sea salt
3 tbsp olive oil
250ml sweet sherry

FOR THE MINT SAUCE
2 tsp caster sugar
½ tsp ground cumin
6 tbsp white wine vinegar
4 tbsp finely chopped mint

Heat the oven to 160°C/140°C fan/gas 3.

Put the onions in the bottom of a large deep-sided casserole or roasting tray if you don't have a casserole big enough to fit the leg of lamb in. Sit the lamb on top of the onions.

Blend together the garlic, rosemary, thyme, lemon zest, paprika, salt and olive oil to give a thick paste.

Spread the paste all over the lamb and put into the oven for 45 minutes.

Pour the sherry over the lamb and baste the lamb with the liquor in the bottom of the casserole or tray. Return to the oven and cook for a further 3 hours, basting the lamb every 45 minutes–1 hour. If the liquid is evaporating, add some water.

While the lamb is cooking, make the mint sauce. Dissolve the sugar in 3 tablespoons of boiling water. Mix in the cumin and vinegar. Just before serving add the chopped mint so it retains its bright green colour.

Remove the dish/tray from the oven and transfer the lamb to a board, ready to carve.

Pour off some of the lamb fat/oil from the cooking liquor, strain the liquor into a jug and serve with the lamb.

Salt-baked celeriac with hazelnut butter

If you've not cooked a celeriac like this before then it is well worth a go – when it is served up at the table it makes a fun centrepiece to crack into. *(See image on following pages.)*

Serves: 6
Preparation time: 20 minutes
Cooking time: 2 hours

1 medium-large celeriac
100g hazelnuts, skin-on
20g extra virgin olive oil
½ tsp sea salt

FOR THE SALT DOUGH
150g rock salt
150g plain flour, plus extra for rolling
1 egg white
2 tbsp chopped rosemary

Preheat the oven to 180°C/160°C fan/gas 4.

To make the salt dough, mix together all of the ingredients to form a pliable dough. Add a little cold water if required. Roll out to approximately 5mm thick on a lightly floured surface. The size of the dough needs to be big enough to cover the celeriac.

Lightly trim the base and top of the celeriac and scrub the outside thoroughly. Wrap in the salt dough and sit on a baking tray. Bake in the oven for 2 hours. Check the celeriac is cooked by inserting a skewer through to the centre – if it feels soft, remove from the oven, but if not cook for longer.

While the celeriac is cooking, scatter the hazelnuts on a baking tray and lightly toast in the oven for 10 minutes. Remove and set aside to cool.

Tip the toasted and cooled hazelnuts into a blender or food processor with the oil and salt. Blend until you have a smooth, thick purée. Taste and add a little more seasoning, if you like.

Crack open the salt dough and scoop the soft celeriac into a bowl. Mix with the hazelnut butter and it is ready to serve.

Slow-cooked smoked beef short rib

You'll need to allow plenty of time for this recipe as the brining, smoking and cooking are all slow processes that can't be rushed – but believe me, the end result is well worth the wait. A full-bodied red wine is the perfect drink to accompany these melt-in-the-mouth ribs.

Serves: 4–6
Preparation time: 30 minutes, plus
   24 hours brining
Cooking time: 8 hours, including
   2 hours smoking

2kg beef short ribs
150g rock salt
150g uncooked rice
25g tea leaves

FOR THE BRINE
100g table salt
1 tbsp white peppercorns
1 tbsp coriander seeds
1 tbsp fennel seeds
3 bay leaves
few sprigs of thyme

FOR THE BRAISING LIQUOR
1 tbsp vegetable oil
1 onion, halved
1 carrot, halved
1 leek, white part only, halved
1 garlic bulb, halved
few sprigs of rosemary
few sprigs of thyme
2 bay leaves
1 bottle red wine
1 star anise
600ml Beef or veal Stock (page 270)
600ml Chicken Stock (page 270)
50g black treacle
1 tbsp Marmite
1 tbsp red wine vinegar

To make the brine, put all of the ingredients and 500ml of water in a large saucepan and bring to the boil. Remove from the heat, add 2 litres of cold water and leave to cool. When cold, add the short ribs and leave them in the brine for 24 hours.

Preheat the oven to 150°C/130°C fan/gas 2 (avoid using the fan oven). Remove the ribs from the brine, rinse under cold water and pat dry. Discard the brine.

Put the rock salt, rice and tea in a large roasting tray lined with foil. Sit a wire rack on top, one that is a similar size to the baking tray, making sure the bottom of the wire isn't touching the rice. Place the ribs on top.

Cover the entire wire rack and tray with a tent of foil, making sure no smoke will escape. Place over high heat for 5 minutes to start the smoking process. Transfer to the lower rack in the oven, removing all other racks, and leave to smoke for 2 hours.

When the ribs are smoked, remove from the oven and discard the rice.

To make the braising liquor, heat the oil in a large pan over medium heat. Add the onion, carrot, leek, garlic and fresh herbs. Brown the vegetables for a few minutes, then pour in the wine. Bring to the boil and reduce by half.

Add the remaining braising liquor ingredients and the smoked ribs. Bring to a gentle simmer, cover and cook over very low heat for 6 hours until the ribs are really tender. Once cooked, remove the ribs from the cooking liquor and keep warm.

Strain the liquor into a clean wide pan and bring to a rapid boil. Reduce until you have a loose glaze consistency. Serve the liquor spooned over the ribs.

Steak with peppercorn sauce and homemade chips

Choose whichever cut you like – rump, sirloin, fillet, onglet – but for me it has to be ribeye, cooked rare, with a spicy peppercorn sauce. Serve with some homemade chips and some sort of salad.

Serves: 4
Preparation time: 15 minutes
Cooking time: 30 minutes

4 boneless ribeye steaks
50ml olive oil
50g butter, diced
2 sprigs of thyme
1 small sprig of rosemary
1 bay leaf
2 garlic cloves, crushed
sea salt and freshly ground black pepper

FOR THE SAUCE
50g unsalted butter
6 shallots, finely chopped
¼ bunch of thyme, leaves picked
1 tbsp Dijon mustard
1 tbsp wholegrain mustard
75ml brandy
75ml ruby port
100ml Beef Stock (page 270)
300g crème fraîche
4 tsp brined green peppercorns, drained
   and roughly chopped

FOR THE CHIPS
6–8 large King Edward potatoes, peeled
   and chipped
sunflower or vegetable oil for deep
   frying

Take the steaks out of the fridge about 1 hour before you want to cook them, to allow them to come to room temperature.

To make the sauce, melt the butter in a frying pan over medium heat, add the shallots, thyme and salt and pepper and cook until the shallots are soft but not coloured.

Increase the heat, stir in both mustards, then pour in the brandy. Stir with a wooden spoon to deglaze, loosening and incorporating any sediment from the bottom of the pan. Simmer to reduce to a syrup consistency, add the port and then simmer further to reduce to a syrup again.

Pour in the stock, bring to the boil, then stir in the crème fraîche and peppercorns. Return to a simmer, add a little more seasoning, if you like, and set aside somewhere warm.

To make the chips, bring a large pan of salted water to the boil. Place the chipped potatoes in the boiling water and gently simmer for 6–8 minutes until just tender. Drain and lay on a clean cloth to dry and cool slightly.

Meanwhile, to cook the steak, heat the oil in a large frying pan. When the oil is smoking, season the ribeye and sear until deep golden on both sides.

Add the butter a cube at a time, until melted and foaming, then add the herbs and garlic. Use a spoon to baste the steak in the butter until the steak is cooked to your liking – for rare, about 4 minutes in total, 7 minutes for medium. Remove the steaks from the pan and set aside to rest for 5 minutes.

Meanwhile, to fry the chips, put the oil in a deep-fat fryer or deep saucepan and heat to 180°C. Lower the chips into the hot oil and fry for 2–3 minutes until deep golden and crisp. Shake off any excess oil and season with sea salt.

Serve topped with the warm peppercorn sauce and the chips alongside.

Home-smoked sea trout with parsnip slaw and pickled pear

Smoking your own fish is something that you may think isn't worth the effort, but believe me, once you taste it there's no going back. This recipe could quite easily sit in the Entertaining chapter as it's really quite impressive, but I think it works nicely as a starter to a Sunday lunch or even as a light supper.

Serves: 4 or 6 as a starter
Preparation time: 30 minutes, plus
   1 hour curing
Cooking time: 20 minutes, plus
   10 minutes smoking

4 skin-on pin-boned rainbow sea
   trout fillets
200–300g rock salt
150g sea salt
150g uncooked rice
25g camomile tea leaves

FOR THE PEARS
150ml white wine vinegar
25g caster sugar
1 tsp juniper berries, lightly crushed
½ tsp coriander seeds
2 ripe pears, cored and diced into 1cm
   pieces

FOR THE SLAW
2 parsnips, coarsely grated
100g crème fraîche
75g mayonnaise
25g hot horseradish sauce
1 tsp wholegrain mustard
1 tbsp honey
50ml milk
¼ grated nutmeg
1 tbsp chopped flat-leaf parsley
1 tbsp chopped tarragon
sea salt and freshly ground black pepper

Weigh the sea trout fillets; for every 100g fish you will need 25g rock salt. Sit the trout in a dish and sprinkle over the rock salt. Leave in the fridge for 1 hour to cure.

Rinse the salted trout in cold water and pat dry with kitchen paper.

Put the sea salt, rice and tea in a roasting tray lined with foil. Sit a wire rack on top, one that is a similar size to the baking tray, making sure the bottom of the wire isn't touching the rice. Lay the salted trout on top, in a single layer.

Cover the entire wire rack and tray with a tent of foil, making sure no smoke will escape. Sit on the hob over medium-low heat for 5 minutes.

Meanwhile, heat the oven to 110°C/90°C fan/gas ¼. Once the trout has smoked, transfer to a baking tray and put in the oven for 5 minutes.

To pickle the pears, bring all of the ingredients except the pears to the boil for 5 minutes in a saucepan. Remove from the heat and add the diced pear. Leave to cool.

To make the parsnip slaw, mix everything together and season to taste.

Flake the smoked sea trout onto plates, serve with the parsnip slaw and a spoon of pickled pears.

Grilled sea bream with lentils and green herb salsa

Sea bream is a versatile fish with tender, succulent flesh. Here I am keeping it really simple by rubbing in olive oil and grilling the fish until the skin is crisp and golden. The hearty braised lentils and robust green herb salsa make this into a well-rounded dish that's perfect for a relaxed Friday night in.

Serves: 4
Preparation time: 20 minutes
Cooking time: 25 minutes

250g Puy lentils
few sprigs of thyme
2 garlic cloves, lightly crushed
vegetable oil, to drizzle
4 skin-on pin-boned and scored sea
  bream fillets
25g pitted green olives, diced
4 anchovy fillets, diced
1 tbsp fine capers
chopped parsley, to serve

FOR THE SALSA
25g anchovy fillets
40g capers
1 tbsp Dijon mustard
150g pitted green olives
2 heaped tbsp finely chopped flat-leaf
  parsley leaves
1 heaped tbsp finely chopped mint leaves
1 heaped tbsp finely chopped basil leaves
100ml olive oil
1 tbsp red wine vinegar
sea salt and freshly ground black pepper

Rinse the lentils and put in a medium-large saucepan. Cover with about three times their volume in water. Add the thyme sprigs, garlic and a good pinch of salt. Bring to the boil and simmer for 15 minutes, until just tender. Remove from the heat and allow to cool for 10 minutes in the cooking liquid, then drain.

To make the green herb salsa, put most of the ingredients in a blender or food processor, leaving a few of the olives, anchovies, capers and a little of the parsley to one side. Pulse, taste and add a little more seasoning, if you like.

Preheat the grill to its highest setting. Drizzle a little vegetable oil over the sea bream fillets, season with salt and rub all over. Place under the grill, skin-side up, for about 6 minutes, until the skin is golden and crisp. Remove from the grill and leave the fish to carry on cooking for a couple of minutes from the heat of the tray.

Toss the warm lentils in enough of the green herb salsa to lightly coat them and spoon onto plates. Place the fish to the side and scatter with the remaining olives, anchovies, capers and chopped parsley. Serve the remaining green herb salsa on the side.

Baked plaice with lemongrass, coriander and green chilli

There is no simpler way of cooking plaice than baking and steaming it in a greaseproof parcel with a few additional ingredients. This is a subtly flavoured fish that is delicious steamed with delicate Asian aromatics. I'd suggest simply serving with an Asian slaw and sweet potato chunks.

Serves: 2
Preparation time: 10 minutes
Cooking time: 20 minutes

2 whole plaice, cleaned (ask your fishmonger to trim them for you)
1 tbsp fish sauce
1 tsp brown sugar
grated zest and juice of 1 lime, plus extra to serve
½ bunch of coriander, plus extra to serve
1 green chilli, finely diced, including seeds
2 lemongrass stalks, bashed

Preheat the oven to 180°C/160°C fan/gas 4.

Cut 2 large pieces of baking parchment at least twice the size of each plaice. Using the tip of a sharp knife, score each side of the plaice skin. Sit each fish on a piece of parchment.

Mix together the fish sauce, sugar, lime zest and juice. Sprinkle over each of the plaice. Scatter over the coriander, chilli and add a lemongrass stalk. Fold up the sides of the parchment to create a parcel and seal by tightly scrunching the edges together (alternatively, if the paper doesn't hold, staple the parcel closed).

Sit each parcel on a baking tray and bake for 15 minutes. Remove from the oven and allow the fish to rest for 5 minutes before opening up the parcel. To check the plaice is cooked, make an incision into the thickest part of the fish and see if the flesh pulls away from the bone. If not, return to the oven for a further 5 minutes. Serve the baked plaice with all of the juices and some lime quarters and coriander scattered over.

TIP: To check the fish is cooked, insert a knife into the centre of the fish, either side of the backbone. If the flesh falls away from the bone, the fish is cooked.

Fishcakes with roast garlic aioli and salsa verde

For the ultimate crisp and crunchy fishcakes with a soft fluffy centre you need to make sure the potatoes are really dry before you combine them with the remaining ingredients. To achieve this, steam rather than boil the potatoes before mashing. Once everything is mixed together, the fishcakes need a thick coating of breadcrumbs to seal everything in, and 10 minutes in the fridge before frying.

Serves: 4
Preparation time: 30 minutes
Cooking time: 30 minutes

2 shallots, roughly chopped
1 garlic clove, crushed
250ml white wine
vegetable oil, for drizzling and shallow-frying
750g skin-on cod, haddock or salmon fillet
500g King Edward potatoes, cut into 3cm chunks
grated zest of 1 lemon
½ red chilli, deseeded and finely chopped
3 spring onions, finely chopped
2 tsp Dijon mustard
1 tbsp chopped flat-leaf parsley
sea salt and freshly ground black pepper
Roast Garlic Aioli (page 272), to serve
Salsa Verde (page 276), to serve

FOR THE CRUMB
75g plain flour, seasoned with salt and pepper
2 eggs, beaten
100g dried breadcrumbs

Put the shallots, garlic and wine into a saucepan and bring to the boil. Allow to reduce in quantity until you have about 3 tablespoons of liquid remaining.

Preheat the oven to 190°C/170°C fan/gas 5 and grease a baking tray with oil. Place the fish, skin-side down, on the oiled baking tray, season and drizzle with a little oil. Roast for 10 minutes, until the fish flakes easily but remains moist. Leave to cool, then remove the skin and flake the fish into a bowl, removing any bones.

Put the potatoes into a steamer set above a pan of boiling water. Steam for 15–20 minutes, until tender. Use a potato ricer or masher to mash the potatoes well.

Add the mashed potatoes to the flaked fish along with the lemon zest, chilli, spring onions, Dijon mustard, parsley, reserved wine reduction and seasoning. Gently mix together and form the mixture into eight cakes. Chill in the fridge for about 20 minutes to firm up.

Coat the fishcakes in the seasoned flour, then egg and finish with a generous coating of breadcrumbs. Return to the fridge for a further 10 minutes.

Pour enough oil into a non-stick frying pan to come up to about 1cm and place over medium heat. Fry the fishcakes for 4 minutes per side, using a spoon to baste them frequently with the hot oil. Lift out with a fish slice, drain and serve sprinkled with salt and pepper and serve with Garlic Aioli and Salsa Verde.

Prawns with prawn butter, sweetcorn and cornbread

This recipe came about when I'd been making prawn butter for the Prawn Orzo Risotto with Monkfish (see page 206) for some friends, which requires prawn shells to make the prawn bisque and butter. That itself is a divine dish, but it left me with lots of peeled prawns. Some went in the freezer for another time, but the rest were used to make this fantastic little recipe.

Serves: 4
Preparation time: 35 minutes
Cooking time: 25 minutes

300g tinned sweetcorn, drained, or frozen
25g unsalted butter
100ml milk
½ tsp sea salt, plus extra
1 whole corncob, husks removed
16 large prawns, peeled and veins removed
75g Prawn Butter (page 276), at room temperature
½ loaf of Cornbread, cut into 2cm cubes (page 242)
¼ red chilli, deseeded and finely chopped

Put the tinned or frozen sweetcorn in a saucepan with the butter, milk and salt. Bring to a gentle simmer and cook for 10 minutes. Remove from the heat and blend to a smooth purée. If preferred, pass through a sieve for a completely smooth consistency. Keep hot.

Bring a pan of salted water to the boil and cook the whole corn for 5 minutes, until just tender. Drain.

Preheat the oven to 220°C/200°C fan/gas 7.

Heat a grill pan over high heat until smoking. Add the whole corn and chargrill all over.

Season the prawns with a pinch of salt and put on the grill pan until almost cooked through and lightly coloured.

Put the prawns, prawn butter and cornbread in a baking tray and place in the oven for about 4 minutes to melt the butter into the prawns and heat the bread through. As you remove the tray from the oven, toss everything together.

Spoon the hot corn purée on to serving plates and spoon over the buttered prawns and cornbread. Cut the chargrilled corn from the cob and scatter over the top with the chilli. Drizzle over any remaining prawn butter from the tray and serve straight away.

Fish pie

Fish pie is a firm favourite in my house, and even though the type of fish or accompaniment might change, we pretty much use the same failsafe recipe every time. This makes a fairly large quantity, so I like to make one larger pie to cook straight away and a couple of individual portions in smaller dishes for the freezer.

Serves: 6
Preparation time: 45 minutes
Cooking time: 1 hour

1kg fish fillets (a mix of salmon and cod or haddock), skinned
600–800ml milk
2 bay leaves
75g butter
1 small onion, diced
1 leek, white part only, sliced
50g plain flour
100ml white wine or white vermouth
2 tbsp crème fraîche
150g frozen peas, defrosted
300g raw tiger prawns, peeled and veins removed
2 tbsp chopped flat-leaf parsley
3 hard-boiled eggs, peeled and chopped
2 tbsp capers
sea salt and freshly ground black pepper

FOR THE TOPPING
1.2kg potatoes, cut to equal-sized chunks
50g butter
splash of milk
100g grated Cheddar cheese

To make the topping, put the potatoes in a large saucepan, cover with cold water, add a pinch of salt and bring to the boil. Cook for 15–20 minutes until cooked through. Drain well and mash in the pan with the butter and a splash of milk until you have smooth, spreadable mash. Season with salt and set aside.

Preheat the oven to 200°C/180°C fan/gas 6.

Next, put the fish fillets in a large pan and add enough milk to cover the fish. Add the bay leaves, a pinch of salt and black pepper. Place over medium heat and gently bring to the boil. Reduce the heat and simmer for 5 minutes until the fish is just cooked through. Remove from the heat.

Melt a third of the butter in a large non-stick saucepan and gently sauté the onion and leek until softened but not coloured. Remove from the pan and set aside.

Return the pan to the heat and add the remaining butter. Once it has melted and is bubbling, stir in the flour. Cook out for about 30 seconds, then add the wine or vermouth. Stir – you should have a thick paste – and return the onion and leeks to the pan.

Strain the milk from the fish fillets into a measuring jug, discarding the bay leaves, and gradually add just 600ml milk to the sauce, stirring until the sauce just coats the back of the spoon. Stir in the crème fraîche and add a little more seasoning, if you like.

Flake the fish into pieces and gently fold into the sauce along with the peas, prawns and parsley.

Spoon the fish pie mixture into one large ovenproof dish (or individual dishes), filling it by about 5cm in depth. Sprinkle over the chopped egg and the capers. Finish with the mashed potato, spreading it over the top with a palette knife. If you like, roughen up the surface with a fork. Finally, sprinkle with cheese and bake for about 20 minutes until the top is golden and the sauce is piping hot.

Falafel with lemon and coriander yoghurt

You'll often see falafel recipes using pre-cooked chickpeas, however, for more authenticity and a better texture, I'm using raw soaked ones. The crisp, golden falafel are packed with herbs and spices, so the fragrant yoghurt makes the perfect accompaniment along with some flatbread, too.

Serves: 4
Preparation time: 10 minutes, plus
   30 minutes chilling
Cooking time: 20 minutes

3 tbsp cumin seeds
1½ tbsp coriander seeds
½ tsp white peppercorns
150g dried chickpeas, soaked in cold
   water overnight
100g podded broad beans
2 shallots, finely diced
½ bunch of flat-leaf parsley, leaves
   picked
½ bunch of coriander, leaves picked
grated zest and juice of 1 lemon
¼ tsp chilli powder
¼ tsp bicarbonate of soda
vegetable oil, for shallow-frying
sea salt

FOR THE YOGHURT
100g caster sugar
1 lemon, thinly sliced and seeds removed
½ bunch of coriander, leaves finely
   chopped
200g unsweetened Greek yoghurt
½ tsp sea salt
1 green chilli, finely chopped

TO SERVE
cucumber, sliced
radishes, quartered
flatbreads

To make the yoghurt, put the sugar and 200ml of water in a saucepan and bring to the boil. Add the lemon slices and simmer for 5 minutes, until translucent. Remove with a slotted spoon and leave to cool.

When the lemon slices are cool, finely chop and mix with the remaining yoghurt ingredients.

To make the falafel, toast the cumin, coriander and peppercorns in a dry frying pan for up to 1 minute until aromatic. Grind to a powder in a spice grinder or pestle and mortar, then tip into a food processor.

Drain the chickpeas and add to the spices in the food processor along with the broad beans, shallots, parsley, coriander, lemon zest and juice, chilli powder, bicarbonate of soda and season with salt. Blitz to a thick paste.

Heat a frying pan with some oil and fry a little of the falafel mixture. Taste and add more seasoning, if you like. Chill the falafel mix in the fridge for 30 minutes to firm up.

Use two tablespoons to shape the falafels into oval-shaped balls.

Pour enough oil to come up to 5cm of the inside of a deep pan. Heat to about 180°C (use a thermometer). Alternatively, drop in a cube of bread and if it becomes crisp and golden within 1 minute the oil is ready.

Fry the falafel in batches for a few minutes until golden on the outside. Drain on kitchen paper and serve with the lemon and coriander yoghurt, cucumber, radishes and flatbreads.

Homemade tagliatelle

When it comes to making your own pasta, this can be a really satisfying job and a great one to get other members of the family involved with, too. I always like to make more dough than I need for just one recipe, as it works better making it in a larger quantity, giving you an egg-rich, silky dough. The leftovers will keep in the fridge for a couple of days, or you can freeze it. *(See step-by-step technique on following pages.)*

Makes: about 900g (serving approx.
  8 portions)
Preparation time: 1 hour, plus at least
  1 hour resting
Cooking time: 2–3 minutes

550g '00' pasta flour, plus extra for
  dusting
3 tsp sea salt
4 large eggs
4 large egg yolks
2 tbsp olive oil

Put the flour and 1 teaspoon of salt in a food processor. In a jug, beat together the whole eggs and egg yolks. Pour about a third of the egg mixture into the food processor. Pulse to combine and, with the motor running, add the oil, then slowly pour in the eggs to get a coarse, crumbly texture. Use your hands to squeeze a small amount of the mixture; if it doesn't come together well, add a little more egg.

Turn the dough out onto a lightly floured work surface. It will be crumbly, but start to bring it together to form a soft ball. Knead well until it is smooth, silky and matt in texture.

Wrap the dough in clingfilm and leave to rest in the fridge for at least 1 hour.

Once the dough has rested it is ready to roll. Divide in half and roll each piece into a strip that is roughly the same width as your pasta machine. Lightly dust the dough and machine with flour and roll each one through the machine. Start with the thickest setting and work your way down to the lowest setting, sprinkling with flour as you go. Repeat this a few times until you have very smooth, thin and even sheets of pasta. If the pasta sheets become too long to handle, cut them into two shorter lengths before the next rolling.

Finally, use the tagliatelle setting and roll the pasta sheets through. Hang the tagliatelle ribbons on a clean broom handle laid horizontally between work surfaces or a table to prevent sticking while you roll the remaining dough.

To cook the tagliatelle, bring a large pan of water to a rapid boil. Add the remaining 2 teaspoons of salt and immediately drop in your chosen quantity of pasta, taking care not to overcrowd the pan. Stir, cover with a lid and return to the boil. Remove the lid and boil for 2–3 minutes, stirring occasionally. Drain well and toss in olive oil to prevent sticking before combining with your chosen sauce or pesto.

Making tagliatelle

Three pestos

Pesto is fantastic if it's freshly made and eaten straight away, and it makes the perfect sauce/dressing for freshly made tagliatelle (see page 142). Traditional basil and pine nut pesto is great, but you can experiment with many different flavours.

Rocket and pumpkin seed

Serves: 6
Preparation time: 10 minutes

125g rocket
60g grated Parmesan cheese
60g pumpkin seeds
200ml olive oil
sea salt and freshly ground black pepper

Put the rocket, Parmesan and pumpkin seeds in a blender or food processor and pulse-blend to roughly chop.

Add the oil and continue to pulse-blend until you have a chunky paste. Season and serve.

Thyme and cobnut

Serves: 4
Preparation time: 20 minutes

300g fresh cobnuts (or hazelnuts)
150–200ml olive oil, plus extra if needed
50g grated Parmesan cheese
15g picked thyme leaves
sea salt and freshly ground black pepper

Remove the husks and shells from the cobnuts and weigh 100g of the nuts to use in the pesto.

Put in a food processor or blender along with 150ml of the oil, the Parmesan, thyme and the seasoning. Pulse-blend until you have a chunky pesto consistency. Add a little more seasoning if you like and add more oil if required.

Tomato and rosemary

Serves: 4
Preparation time: 20 minutes, plus cooling
Cooking time: 2 hours

10 ripe plum tomatoes or 100g semi-dried
150ml olive oil, plus extra for drizzling
2 garlic cloves, finely sliced
2 tbsp finely chopped rosemary
50g toasted pine nuts
50g grated Parmesan cheese
sea salt and freshly ground black pepper

Preheat the oven to 120°C/100°C fan/gas ½.

Cut the tomatoes into quarters, remove the seeds and sit in a single layer, cut-side up on a baking sheet. Drizzle lightly with olive oil and sprinkle with the sliced garlic. Season with salt and bake for about 2 hours, until semi-dried.

Remove from the oven and leave to cool. Put in a blender or food processor with the rosemary, pine nuts and Parmesan. Pulse-blend to roughly chop, then gradually add the oil until you have a chunky pesto consistency. Season to taste and serve.

Harissa-glazed aubergine with coconut and peanuts

Aubergines are a fantastic vegetable that absorb flavours really well. They do release a lot of liquid when cooked, though, so it's important to chargrill the slices until really golden, otherwise the additional flavours will become diluted when serving.

Serves: 4
Preparation time: 20 minutes
Cooking time: 30 minutes

2 aubergines
3 tbsp olive or rapeseed oil
1 tsp flaked sea salt, plus extra
150g dairy-free coconut yoghurt
grated zest and juice of 1 lime
50g rose harissa
30g agave syrup
1 tsp lemon juice
75g roasted and salted peanuts, roughly
   chopped
½–1 red chilli, finely sliced
coriander cress or salad cress

Preheat the oven to 200°C/180°C fan/gas 6. Heat a chargrill pan until hot.

Slice each aubergine lengthways into six long strips. Brush with the oil and season with the salt.

Chargrill both sides of the aubergine slices until deep golden. You may need to do this in a couple of batches depending on the size of your pan.

Transfer to a foil-lined baking tray and finish cooking in the oven for 15 minutes.

Mix together the coconut yoghurt, lime zest and juice, and a good pinch of salt. Set aside.

Mix together the harissa, agave syrup, 4 teaspoons of water and lemon juice. Season with salt and when the aubergine is cooked, brush liberally over the top of each strip. Return to the oven for 5 minutes.

To serve, place the aubergine slices on a large plate and dot the coconut yoghurt around. Scatter over the peanuts, chilli and cress.

Ricotta and semi-dried tomato gnocchi with piquillo pepper sauce

Homemade gnocchi needn't be difficult at all, but it is important to allow the ricotta to 'hang' for a good few hours to drain off excess moisture. You can do this in muslin cloth or by using a fine sieve – either will suffice if left long enough.

Serves: 4
Preparation time: 50 minutes, plus at
  least 8 hours draining
Cooking time: 10–20 minutes

400g ricotta cheese
100g semi-dried tomatoes, finely
  chopped
125g plain flour
125g fine semolina, plus extra for rolling
1 large egg, lightly beaten
½ tsp smoked paprika
1 tbsp finely chopped flat-leaf parsley
  leaves
olive oil, for frying
40g baby spinach leaves
Parmesan cheese, to serve

FOR THE SAUCE
1 tbsp olive oil
1 garlic clove, crushed
2 small ripe tomatoes, about the size of
  golf balls, roughly chopped
100g piquillo peppers, from a jar,
  drained and roughly chopped
50ml white wine
½ tsp red wine vinegar
½ tsp caster sugar
1 heaped tsp roughly chopped oregano
sea salt and freshly ground black pepper

To make the gnocchi, put the ricotta cheese in a fine sieve set over a bowl. Cover with clingfilm and keep in the fridge for at least 8 hours or overnight to drain off any excess liquid.

Put the drained ricotta in a mixing bowl with the semi-dried tomatoes, flour, semolina, beaten egg, smoked paprika and parsley and season with salt and pepper. Mix together until you have a soft dough, adding a little more flour if the dough feels sticky when poked.

Roll the dough into small balls, weighing about 10g each, and lightly coat in semolina. Roll a fork over them to create a classic gnocchi shape, and keep cool until you are ready to cook them.

To make the sauce, heat the oil in a small-medium saucepan and add the garlic. Cook for 30 seconds, add the tomatoes and allow to simmer for 3 minutes, until they are softened. Stir in the peppers, white wine, red wine vinegar, sugar and oregano. Bring to the boil and simmer for 5 minutes to reduce the wine by half.

Transfer to a blender, or use a stick blender, and blitz until smooth. Season to taste.

Lightly oil a steamer and arrange the gnocchi inside. Set above a pan of simmering water, cover and cook for 5 minutes. (You may need to do this in batches depending on the size of your steamer.)

Heat a drizzle of oil in a large frying pan. Toss in the spinach and when it starts to wilt, add the sauce and then heat through. Add the cooked gnocchi and toss in the pan to coat well in the sauce.

Spoon onto plates and finish with shavings of Parmesan cheese.

Risotto with courgette, ricotta and peas

The idea for this light and summery risotto came about when I had some leftover ravioli filling mix. I stirred it through a plain risotto base and, I think you'll agree, it not only tastes really delicious but looks great, too.

Serves: 4
Preparation time: 20 minutes
Cooking time: 20–25 minutes

250g courgette, grated
150g ricotta cheese
175g frozen peas, defrosted
½ red chilli, finely chopped
2 tbsp chopped coriander
grated zest of ½ lemon
approx. 1.3 litres Chicken or Vegetable
   Stock (pages 270–1)
3 tbsp vegetable oil
2 shallots, finely chopped
1 garlic clove, chopped
500g Carnaroli or Vialone Nano
   risotto rice
good splash of dry white wine
75g Parmesan cheese, grated
sea salt and freshly ground black pepper
handful of pea shoots, to serve
extra virgin olive oil, to serve

Put the grated courgette in a clean tea towel and squeeze out any excess moisture. Transfer to a bowl and mix with the ricotta, peas, chilli, coriander and lemon zest. Season with salt and pepper and set aside.

Put the stock in a saucepan and bring to the boil. Reduce the heat and leave to gently simmer.

Heat the oil in a deep frying pan over medium heat, add the shallots and garlic, and cook for a few minutes until the shallots have softened but not coloured.

Add the rice and stir around in the pan for a few minutes until it becomes shiny and translucent. When it starts to make a faint popping sound, add the wine and let it reduce away, stirring continuously.

Add a ladleful of the hot stock, season and stir. Simmer and continue stirring until the stock has been absorbed. Add the remaining stock a ladleful at a time, stirring continuously until each ladleful has been absorbed before adding the next, about 15–20 minutes. The risotto is cooked when the rice grains are a little firm but don't have any chalky crunch on the outside when bitten into.

Stir in the courgette, ricotta and pea mixture and allow the risotto to come to a simmer. Finally, stir in most of the Parmesan, adding any extra stock if required.

Taste, add a little more seasoning if you like and serve straight away, garnished with a few pea shoots, the remaining Parmesan and a drizzle of extra virgin olive oil.

Pizza

The beauty of homemade pizza is that you can customise the basic tomato sauce with a variety of toppings and alter them depending on who it is for. You should also consider using a number of toppings separated into sections on one large rectangular pizza, which can then be sliced to suit everyone's tastes. *(See image on previous pages.)*

Makes: 1 large or a selection of smaller ones
Preparation time: 30 minutes, plus 1 hour for rising
Cooking time: 55 minutes

FOR THE DOUGH
500g strong white bread flour, plus extra for dusting
7g sachet fast-action dried yeast
1 tsp sugar
1 tsp sea salt
25ml olive oil

FOR THE TOMATO SAUCE
2 tbsp olive oil
1 onion, sliced
1 garlic clove, crushed
1 × 400g tin chopped tomatoes
2 tbsp tomato purée
2 tbsp balsamic vinegar
1 tbsp light brown sugar
1 tbsp sweet chilli sauce
½ tsp dried oregano
1 tbsp chopped flat-leaf parsley leaves
sea salt and freshly ground black pepper

To make the dough, put the flour in a large bowl and stir in the yeast, sugar and salt. Make a well in the centre and pour in 300ml of warm water and the oil. Mix together until you have a smooth, wet dough. Turn onto a lightly floured surface and knead for 5 minutes. Alternatively, make the dough in a standmixer fitted with a dough hook.

Transfer to a clean, lightly oiled bowl, cover with oiled clingfilm and leave in a warm place to double in volume.

To make the sauce, heat the oil in a saucepan and add the onion and garlic. Cook for 10 minutes over medium-low heat until golden. Add the remaining sauce ingredients, season with salt and pepper and bring to a simmer. Cook for 30 minutes, stirring occasionally. Transfer to a blender or use a stick blender to blitz the sauce to a smooth consistency, then set aside to cool.

Preheat the oven to 220°C/200°C fan/gas 7. Put a baking tray in the oven to heat up.

Turn out the risen dough onto a floured surface and knead for a couple of minutes. Roll to your desired shape and thickness, or make smaller pizzas and place on a lightly floured baking tray.

Spread a layer of tomato sauce on the base, leaving a 2cm border, and carefully slide the pizza onto the hot tray in the oven.

Bake in the oven for about 10 minutes until the base is crisp. Remove from the oven and add your chosen toppings. Return the pizza to the oven for another 5 minutes until golden.

Topping suggestions. Here are a few of my family's favourite ones…

Pesto, pine nut, mozzarella and black pepper

Makes: 1 large or 2 small
Preparation time: 5 minutes

200g mozzarella, torn or sliced into
   pieces
3–4 tbsp pesto, bought or homemade
   (page 147)
20g toasted pine nuts
sea salt and freshly ground black pepper
olive oil, to drizzle

Arrange the mozzarella on top of the partially cooked tomato-sauce-topped pizza base. Spoon on the pesto and scatter with pine nuts.

Season with salt and plenty of black pepper. Drizzle over a little oil and return to the oven for 5 minutes until golden.

Grated sweet potato, cashew and rocket

Makes: 1 large or 2 small
Preparation time: 10 minutes

1 small sweet potato
olive oil, to drizzle
sea salt and freshly ground black pepper
25g cashew nuts
20g rocket leaves

Peel and grate the sweet potato and put into a clean cloth. Squeeze out the excess water and put into a bowl. Drizzle over a little oil and season. Mix to coat the potato in the oil, then scatter over the top of the partially cooked tomato-sauce-topped pizza base.

Add the cashew nuts and season with salt and black pepper.

Drizzle over a little oil and return to the oven for 5 minutes until golden.

When cooked, top with rocket leaves and serve straight away.

Salami, jalapeno, broccoli and almond

Makes: 1 large or 2 small
Preparation time: 10 minutes

100g Tenderstem broccoli
5–6 slices salami
100g mozzarella, sliced or torn into pieces
2 jalapeno peppers, roughly chopped
2 tbsp flaked almonds
sea salt and freshly ground black pepper
olive oil, to drizzle

Cook the broccoli in a steamer set over a pan of boiling water for 2 minutes, until very lightly cooked. Arrange on the partially cooked tomato-sauce-topped pizza base, along with the salami, pieces of mozzarella, jalapeno peppers and almonds.

Season with salt and black pepper, drizzle over a little oil and return to the oven for 5 minutes until golden.

Lemon fudge puddings

I'm sure most people have a tin of condensed milk in their cupboard, and with the addition of a few other everyday ingredients you can prepare a fantastic dessert in no time at all. The light yet tangy sponge of these simple puddings balances perfectly with the sweet, sticky fudge running through the centre. Finished off with ice cream or crème fraîche, you're in for a real treat.

Makes: 6
Preparation time: 20 minutes
Cooking time: 15 minutes

100g unsalted butter, melted, plus extra
    for greasing
150g caster sugar, plus 2 tbsp extra
2 eggs
grated zest and juice of 2 lemons
125g plain flour
1 tsp baking powder
crème fraîche or vanilla ice cream,
    to serve

FOR THE FUDGE
grated zest and juice of 1 lemon
200g condensed milk

Preheat the oven to 200°C/180°C fan/gas 6.

Lightly butter 6 ramekin dishes and sprinkle evenly with the 2 tablespoons of sugar.

To make the lemon fudge, combine the lemon zest and juice and condensed milk. Set aside.

For the puddings, put the eggs and 150g caster sugar in a mixing bowl and whisk on high speed until light and fluffy.

Stir the butter, lemon zest and juice into the eggs and sugar, then fold in the flour and baking powder.

Put a good spoonful of the pudding mixture into the bottom of the ramekins. Spoon the lemon fudge on top. Finish by spooning the remaining lemon pudding mix over the fudge. Smooth over the surface with a palette knife.

Sit on a baking tray and bake for 15 minutes, until the puddings puff up and become golden.

Leave to rest for a minute or two and serve with a spoonful of crème fraîche or ice cream spooned over the top.

Prune and Armagnac tart

If you are looking for a festive dessert, this is the one to try. The combination of prunes soaked in Armagnac baked into a rich, buttery almond frangipane on top of crisp, sweet pastry is simply delicious.

Serves: 8–10
Preparation time: 40 minutes plus
   5 days soaking and 30 minutes chilling
Cooking time: 1 hour 20 minutes

FOR THE PRUNES
400ml Armagnac
125g caster sugar
peeled zest of ½ lemon
peeled zest of ½ orange
pinch of ground cinnamon
1 tea bag
400g dried ready-to-eat prunes

FOR THE PASTRY
175g plain flour, plus extra for rolling
pinch of sea salt
115g cold butter, diced
50g caster sugar
1 whole egg, beaten
1 egg yolk

FOR THE FRANGIPANE
150g caster sugar
150g soft butter
3 eggs
pinch of sea salt
185g ground almonds

TO SERVE
Vanilla Custard (page 278) or Earl Grey
   Custard (page 279) (optional)

To prepare the prunes, put 250ml of water, the Armagnac, sugar, lemon and orange zests, cinnamon and the tea bag in a saucepan and bring to the boil. Put the prunes in a large bowl. Remove the tea bag from the pan and pour the liquid over the prunes into the bowl. Cover and store in a cool place for 5 days, turning the prunes every so often.

For the pastry, rub together the flour, salt and cold butter until you have a breadcrumb-like texture. Stir in the sugar and gradually add the whole egg to form a soft, pliable dough. Wrap in clingfilm and chill for 30 minutes.

Roll the pastry on a lightly floured surface and use it to line a 23cm loose-bottomed tart tin, leaving a little excess pastry to hang over the edges. Return to the fridge for 20 minutes.

Preheat the oven to 220°C/200°C fan/gas 7. Line the pastry case with baking parchment and fill with baking beans. Sit on a baking sheet and bake for 5 minutes. Reduce the oven temperature to 180°C/160°C fan/gas 4 and bake the tart case for a further 15 minutes, until it starts to turn golden and become firm. Remove the baking beans and parchment, brush with the egg yolk and return to the oven for a further 5 minutes, until evenly golden. Remove and allow to cool slightly. When cool enough to handle, trim away the excess pastry with a sharp knife.

To make the frangipane, beat together the sugar and butter until light and creamy. Add the eggs one at a time, beating well after each addition. Finally mix in the pinch of salt and almonds.

Drain the prunes from the soaking liquid and reserve about 100ml and about 18 of the soaked prunes. Blitz the remaining prunes in a blender or food processor until you have a smooth purée.

Spread the purée on the bottom of the pastry case followed by the frangipane, then arrange the whole prunes on top. Bake for 40–45 minutes, until deep golden and the frangipane has just set in the centre. Cool for at least 15 minutes before brushing with the remaining soaking liquid and serving with Vanilla Custard or Earl Grey Custard, if you like.

Poached pear, burnt honey mascarpone mousse and oat crumble

This is a wonderful dessert of three components, each with a contrasting flavour and texture, but they work so well when combined. The crumble can be made ahead and stored for up to 1 week in a container. As for the pears, if you are pushed for time you could substitute with some decent bought poached pears. *(See image on previous pages.)*

Serves: 8
Preparation time: 45 minutes, plus
   2 hours chilling
Cooking time: 30 minutes

FOR THE PEARS
200g caster sugar
1 tbsp lemon juice
2 star anise, lightly crushed
1 cinnamon stick, lightly crushed
4 whole pears, halved and cored

FOR THE MOUSSE
6 egg yolks
225g honey
2 gelatine leaves
400g mascarpone cheese
100ml double cream

FOR THE CRUMBLE
100g plain flour
30g oats
60g demerara sugar
60g cold butter, diced
pinch of sea salt

TO SERVE
Greek yoghurt or Burnt Honey Custard
   (page 278)

To make the poached pears, place 600ml of water in a saucepan with the sugar, lemon juice and spices. Bring to the boil, add the pears and cover with a circle of greaseproof paper that fits inside the pan. Reduce to a simmer and gently cook for 5–10 minutes until just tender. (The timings depend on the ripeness of the pears.) Remove from the heat and leave to cool. Chill in the fridge until needed.

For the mousse, put the egg yolks in the bowl of a standmixer and whisk until pale and creamy. Bring the honey to a boil in a saucepan over high heat. Cook until it caramelises to a deep golden brown. Slowly whisk the honey into the egg yolks while hot, and keep whisking until the mixture has cooled.

Soak the gelatine in cold water for 5 minutes. Heat 100g of the mascarpone in a small pan. Squeeze the excess water from the gelatine and stir it into the hot mascarpone until completely dissolved. Beat in the remaining mascarpone until smooth and fold into the egg yolk and honey. Lightly whip the double cream to soft peaks and gently fold into the mascarpone mixture. Place in the fridge to chill.

To make the crumble, heat the oven to 200°C/180°C fan/gas 6. Line a baking tray with baking parchment. Pulse-blend all the ingredients in a food processor to a coarse breadcrumb texture. Spread in an even layer on the tray and bake for 20 minutes, until golden and crunchy, turning a few times so it cooks evenly. Set aside to cool.

To assemble, remove the pears from the cooking liquor. Core and slice into long pieces. Divide the diced pears among four bowls. Top with the crumble, a spoonful of Greek yoghurt or Burnt Honey Custard, then the mousse and lay the sliced pear on top. Serve straight away.

Coconut mousse with pineapple and lime

I've been known to enjoy a good cocktail or two, many of which lend themselves to being converted into desserts, such as a Piña Colada. Coconut cream, pineapple and rum are all used here to produce a light, airy, dairy-free mousse topped with a refreshing fruit salad that's a perfect end to a meal with friends.

Serves: 4–6
Preparation time: 30 minutes, plus
  2 hours chilling, plus 6 hours
  marinating
Cooking time: 10 minutes

2 gelatine leaves
100g coconut cream
100g caster sugar
2 egg whites
100g dairy-free coconut yoghurt
2 tsp fresh lime juice

FOR THE PINEAPPLE AND LIME
½ small-medium ripe pineapple
1 tbsp dark rum
grated zest and juice of 1 lime
¼ bunch of mint, leaves finely chopped

Peel and dice the pineapple into ½–1cm pieces. Mix with the rum, the lime zest and juice and the mint and set aside for at least 6 hours, covered.

To make the mousse, soak the gelatine in a bowl of cold water for about 5 minutes until softened. Heat the coconut cream in a small saucepan until hot but not boiling.

Squeeze the excess water from the gelatine and stir the gelatine into the coconut cream, until dissolved. Strain the mixture into a mixing bowl and allow to cool.

Place the sugar and 3 tablespoons of water in a saucepan and set over medium heat. Stir until the sugar dissolves, then bring to a fast boil, until it reaches 110°C on a sugar thermometer.

Whisk the egg whites until they form stiff peaks.

When the syrup temperature reaches 110°C on the sugar thermometer, slowly and carefully pour the syrup over the egg whites in a thin stream while continuing to whisk.

Continue whisking for up to 10 minutes, until the meringue has cooled.

Combine the coconut yoghurt and lime juice with the coconut cream and gelatine. Fold this mixture in the cooled meringue and spoon into four to six serving glasses/dishes.

Chill in the fridge to set for about 2 hours.

To serve, spoon the marinated pineapple on top of the chilled mousse.

Pumpkin and maple custards

A cross between a crème caramel and pumpkin pie, this is an interesting pudding that uses the natural sweetness of a generally savoury ingredient.

Makes 6
Preparation time: 40 minutes, plus
  1 hour cooling and chilling
Cooking time: 20 minutes

6 tbsp maple syrup
200g whipping cream
100g whole milk
½ nutmeg, finely grated
100g egg yolks
80g caster sugar
200g pumpkin purée (delica or kabocha squash, steamed and blended)
25ml whisky
black sesame seeds, to serve
sea salt, to serve

Preheat the oven to 120°C/100°C fan/gas ½. Have ready a deep baking tray with 6 ramekins or ovenproof glass bowls sitting inside. Place 1 tablespoon of maple syrup in the bottom of each ramekin.

Bring the cream and milk to the boil with the nutmeg, then reduce the heat to low. Whisk the yolks and sugar together, then add a little of the hot cream, whisking well. Pour the yolk mix over the hot cream and mix well. Stir with a spatula over a low heat until the mixture begins to coat the back of a spoon.

Mix in the pumpkin purée, then strain through a fine sieve into a jug. Fill the tray with enough just-boiled water to come to about halfway up the sides of the ramekins. Pour the custard into the ramekins, then cover the entire tray with foil. Very carefully place in the oven for 20 minutes.

Remove the tray carefully from the oven and peel back the foil. To test if the custards are done, remove one of the ramekins, using a hot cloth, and shake it gently to check the wobble. It should wobble only in the centre – if it doesn't, replace the foil and leave to stand for another 10 minutes. When done, remove the ramekins from the water bath and allow to cool for 30 minutes. Place in the fridge to chill completely.

Remove the custards from the fridge at least an hour before serving. Top with sesame seeds and salt and serve.

Summer strawberry 'margarita'

This recipe takes all of the elements from a very popular cocktail and serves them up as a refreshing dessert. It tastes amazing, is exceptionally refreshing and is a real crowd-pleaser.

Serves: 4
Preparation time: 20 minutes plus at least 3 hours freezing

400g ripe strawberries
25ml Cointreau
½ tsp Himalayan pink salt, to serve

FOR THE LIME GRANITA
50g caster sugar
50ml lime juice

FOR THE TEQUILA CREAM
100ml crème fraîche
10g icing sugar
25g good-quality tequila
150ml double cream

To make the lime granita, put 50ml of water in a small saucepan, add the sugar and stir until dissolved. Add the lime juice, pour the mixture into a small shallow metal tray or cake tin and transfer to the freezer for 1 hour.

Use a fork to scrape the mixture and return to the freezer, repeating a couple of times until you have fluffy ice crystals.

To make the tequila cream, simply whisk all of the ingredients together until stiff peaks form.

Remove the stalks from the strawberries and cut any larger ones in half or quarters. Toss in the Cointreau and divide the strawberries between 4 bowls. Remove the granita from the freezer, give it a final scrape with a fork, then spoon on top of the strawberries. Dollop a large spoonful of the tequila cream on top and sprinkle with the pink salt. Serve immediately.

Dark chocolate mousse with salted caramel cream

These chocolate mousses served with a dollop of salted caramel cream on top are extremely moreish and the perfect end to a meal.

Serves: 8
Preparation time: 45 minutes, plus
  2 hours setting
Cooking time: 15 minutes

250ml whipping cream
100ml milk
25g caster sugar
2 egg yolks
180g dark chocolate (minimum 60% cocoa solids), broken into small pieces

FOR THE SALTED CARAMEL CREAM
100g caster sugar
50ml milk
½ tsp sea salt
250ml double cream

Put 150ml of the whipping cream into a saucepan with the milk and bring to the boil.

In a large bowl whisk together the sugar and egg yolks. Pour over the hot milk and cream, mixing well. Return to the saucepan, place over low heat and stir continuously until the custard thickens enough to thickly coat the back of a wooden spoon. If you have a sugar thermometer, cook to 85°C.

Put the chocolate in a bowl, strain the hot custard over the top and stir to melt the chocolate. Leave to cool to room temperature.

Lightly whip the remaining 100ml of whipping cream until it just holds its shape. Fold into the chocolate and divide between 8 ramekins or glasses.

Chill in the fridge for about 2 hours to set, then remove about 20 minutes before serving.

To make the salted caramel cream, put the sugar in a saucepan over medium heat. Leave it to caramelise to a deep golden colour, occasionally shaking the pan, but do not stir at all.

Meanwhile, in a separate pan gently warm the milk, salt and 100ml of the double cream. Pour into the caramelised sugar, whisking to combine. Strain through a sieve and leave to cool.

When the caramel has completely cooled, whisk the remaining 150ml of double cream to soft peaks. Add the cooled caramel and continue to whisk until stiff peaks form.

Spoon the caramel cream on top of the chocolate mousse and serve.

Toasted almond panna cotta

Toasted almonds are infused into the cream and their flavour is intensified with the addition of the caramel-like almond liqueur. If you like almonds, you'll love these.

Serves: 4
Preparation time: 20 minutes, plus
  2 hours infusing and 3 hours chilling
Cooking time: 15 minutes

vegetable oil, for greasing
200g flaked almonds
350ml milk
350ml whipping cream
60g demerara sugar
25ml amaretto
3 gelatine leaves

Preheat the oven to 200°C/180°C fan/gas 6. Lightly oil 4 pudding moulds, rings, ramekins or tea cups.

Put the almonds on a baking sheet and toast in the oven for 10–12 minutes, shaking the tray a couple of times to ensure even colouring, until golden.

Put the milk, cream and sugar in a saucepan and bring to the boil over medium heat.

Remove from the heat and stir in the toasted almonds (reserving a few to scatter over) and the amaretto. Cover the pan with clingfilm and leave to infuse for 2 hours.

Put the mixture in a blender or use a stick blender and blitz until smooth. Pass through a sieve ideally lined with a piece of muslin cloth, however if you don't have this then a fine sieve will also work.

Soak the gelatine in a bowl of cold water for 5 minutes. Take a ladle of the almond cream and heat in a small saucepan. Squeeze the excess water out of the gelatine and stir the gelatine into the pan until dissolved. Add to the remaining almond cream.

Pour the mix into your lightly oiled pudding moulds. Chill in the fridge for about 3 hours, until set.

Carefully turn out the panna cotta from their moulds and serve with the reserved toasted almonds scattered over the top.

ENTERTAINING

Watercress soup with soft-poached egg and mustard crumb

To ensure you retain the wonderful vibrant green colour of the watercress it's essential to chill the soup immediately, as soon as it's cooked. So do make sure you have a bowl of iced water and a sieve at the ready.

I also recommend pre-poaching the eggs and setting them aside in iced water. Then you simply need to reheat them for 2 minutes in simmering water before serving.

Serves: 6 as a starter
Preparation time: 20 minutes
Cooking time: 25 minutes

300g watercress, put a few small sprigs
  in cold water in the fridge to serve
40g unsalted butter
1 mashing potato, very thinly sliced
750ml hot Vegetable or Chicken Stock
  (pages 270–1)
200ml milk
¼ tsp English mustard
olive oil, to serve
sea salt and freshly ground black pepper

FOR THE CRUMB
20g skin-on whole almonds
1 thick slice of day-old bread
20g grated Parmesan cheese
2 tsp wholegrain mustard
15g butter

FOR THE SOFT-POACHED EGGS
4 eggs
½ tsp white wine vinegar

Pick all the leaves from the watercress stalks, chop the stalks into small pieces and roughly chop the leaves. Fill a bowl with ice and water and set another bowl on top – this will help to cool the soup quickly.

Heat the butter in a large saucepan. Add the potato and gently cook until softened but not coloured. Add a few twists of black pepper, salt and 375ml of stock and bring to the boil. Drop in the watercress stalks, return to the boil and cook for 1 minute. Pour in the remaining stock, bring to the boil, then add the watercress leaves. Cover and cook for 3 minutes.

Blitz in a blender or using a stick blender until smooth and pass through a sieve into the bowl inside the iced water bowl. Stir in the milk and mustard, then season. Whisk to mix and chill the soup quicker. When cool, cover and keep in the fridge.

Preheat the oven to 200°C/180°C fan/gas 6 and line a baking sheet with baking parchment. Pulse the mustard crumb ingredients in a food processor to a coarse crumb, then spread in a thin layer on the baking sheet. Bake for 12–15 minutes, turning halfway, until deep golden and crunchy. Leave to cool.

To poach the eggs, boil a large saucepan of water with a good pinch of salt. Crack the eggs into four bowls and add a few drops of vinegar to each. Whisk the boiling water so it swirls in a whirlpool and turn the heat to medium-low – a gentle simmer – then slide in the eggs. Poach for 3 minutes, remove with a slotted spoon and place in iced water. To reheat, place in boiling salted water for 2 minutes.

Heat the soup, then ladle into shallow bowls and sit the eggs on top. Garnish with the reserved watercress sprigs and spoon over the mustard crumb. Finish with a sprinkling of salt, a twist of pepper and a drizzle of olive oil and serve.

Chilled lettuce soup with pickled cucumber and crab

The beauty of this dish is that everything can be prepared ahead and simply assembled when ready to serve, making it a perfect starter recipe when entertaining. As with the Watercress Soup (see page 174), it's essential to chill this soup as soon as it's made to retain the lettuce's vibrant green colour.

Serves: 6 as a starter
Preparation time: 20 minutes, plus
  1 hour pickling
Cooking time: 10 minutes

25g unsalted butter
1 banana shallot, chopped
1 mashing potato, finely sliced
750ml cold Vegetable or Chicken Stock
50g baby spinach
1 iceberg lettuce, core removed and
  finely sliced
squeeze of lemon juice
few walnut pieces, lightly toasted
parsley cress or salad cress, to serve
sea salt and freshly ground black pepper

FOR THE PICKLED CUCUMBER
⅓ cucumber
50ml white wine vinegar
1 tbsp honey

FOR THE CRAB
100g white crab meat
1 tbsp extra virgin olive oil
juice of ½ lime

Heat a large saucepan and melt the butter. Add the shallot and potato. Cook over a gentle heat until the potato has cooked but not coloured.

Pour in half of the stock and bring to the boil. Add the spinach, cook for about 30 seconds and then add the iceberg lettuce. Cook for up to 1 minute until the lettuce is limp.

Fill a bowl with ice and water and set another bowl on top. Quickly blitz the soup in a blender, or using a stick blender, until smooth and pass through a sieve into the bowl inside the iced water bowl. (This will quickly chill the soup, keeping the vibrant green colour.) Stir in the lemon juice and remaining stock. Season and whisk well until cold. Cover and chill in the fridge until needed.

Peel, deseed and finely dice the cucumber. Put in a small bowl and mix with the vinegar and honey. Leave for about 1 hour to pickle.

Mix the crab meat with the olive oil and lime juice. Season to taste.

To serve, ladle the chilled soup into bowls. Divide the crab and pickled cucumber on top and finish with a scattering of walnuts and parsley cress or salad cress.

Warm salad of chicken, baby vegetables and spiced vinaigrette

I love using baby root vegetables when in season, but it's essential not to overcook them or their delicate flavour is lost. I like to blanch them first to take away the rawness, then give them a few minutes in a hot oven for some colour and to heat through, ready to absorb the flavoursome vinaigrette.

Serves: 4–6 as a starter
Preparation time: 30 minutes
Cooking time: 55 minutes

FOR THE CHICKEN
2 garlic bulbs
2 tbsp olive oil
2 skinless chicken breasts
6 sprigs of thyme
100ml Chicken Stock (page 270)

FOR THE VEGETABLES
4 baby fennel bulbs
4 baby carrots, scrubbed
8 baby leeks
8 baby turnips, halved
50ml olive oil
½ garlic bulb, halved
3 sprigs of thyme
2 little gem hearts, leaves separated

FOR THE VINAIGRETTE
½ tsp coriander seeds
4 white peppercorns
½ nutmeg, grated
4 cloves
½ cinnamon stick
1 star anise
2.5cm piece of fresh ginger, peeled and
    grated
100ml white wine vinegar
2 tbsp honey
100ml extra virgin olive oil
2 tbsp finely chopped micro parsley or
    baby cress, plus extra to serve
sea salt and freshly ground black pepper

Preheat the oven to 200°C/180°C fan/gas 6. Place the garlic bulbs on a piece of foil, drizzle with the olive oil and add a good pinch of salt. Wrap and place in the oven for 30 minutes, until the garlic is sticky and golden.

Meanwhile, bring a large saucepan of salted water to the boil and blanch each type of baby vegetable separately until almost cooked through. Remove with a slotted spoon and refresh in iced water. Drain well and pat dry with kitchen paper.

To make the vinaigrette, dry roast the spices and ginger in a saucepan, shaking them around for a minute or so to release their aroma. Add the vinegar and honey. Bring to the boil and cook until the liquid has reduced by half. Strain through a sieve and set aside to cool. When cool, whisk in the extra virgin olive oil and chopped micro parsley or baby cress and season with salt and pepper to taste.

Line a baking tray with foil and place the chicken breasts on top, spaced slightly apart. Season well and squeeze the sticky garlic on top of the chicken. Scatter over the thyme and pour over the stock. Wrap the foil to seal the chicken in and cook in the oven for 20 minutes. Remove from the oven and set aside.

To finish off the vegetables, increase the heat of the oven to 220°C/200°C fan/gas 7. Put the remaining olive oil, garlic bulb and thyme in a roasting tray. Place in the oven for 5 minutes to heat up and for the flavours to infuse the oil. Add the blanched vegetables and the little gem, toss in the oil and cook for about 5 minutes so the vegetables heat through and are lightly golden.

Tip the vegetables into a bowl and drizzle over some vinaigrette. Divide between plates or serve on a large platter with the warm roasted garlic chicken sliced thinly and extra vinaigrette to spoon over and micro parsley or baby cress scattered over.

Duck and pork terrine

You may think a terrine is complicated to prepare but in fact some recipes can be relatively straightforward, and the end result is just as delicious as from more complex versions. This particular terrine is made using a combination of meats, which offers differing flavours and textures that work very well together.

I like to serve this as a starter with some of my homemade Onion Marmalade (see page 275) and toasted sourdough, though any leftovers are particularly good as a late supper with pickles and crusty bread. (*See step-by-step technique on following pages.*)

Serves: 8–10 as a starter
Preparation time: 30 minutes, plus
    overnight chilling
Cooking time: 1½ hours

250ml port
1 skin-on duck breast
500g pork shoulder, diced
200g duck livers, roughly chopped
finely grated zest of 1 orange
2 tsp ground allspice
½ nutmeg, grated
½ tsp ground cinnamon
2 tsp flaked sea salt, plus extra to season
10–12 rashers streaky bacon
freshly ground black pepper
olive oil, for drizzling
chopped pistachio nuts, to serve

TO SERVE
sourdough loaf
Onion Marmalade (page 275)
1 shallot, diced
parsley leaves

Put the port in a small saucepan and bring to the boil. Simmer until reduced to 120ml. Remove from the heat and leave to cool.

Remove the skin from the duck breast, finely dice along with the breast, and put in the bowl of a food processor. Add the pork shoulder and duck livers and pulse to break down the meat until coarsely minced.

Transfer to a large bowl and mix in the reduced port, orange zest, spices, the flaked sea salt and some freshly ground black pepper. Mix well.

Line a 1.1 litre lidded terrine mould or loaf tin with a triple layer of clingfilm, twice the size of the tin.

Lay the bacon rashers on a board and stretch them out, one at a time, using the back of a knife. Place the first rasher horizontally in the tin, slightly overlapped if the bacon is long enough. Repeat with the remaining rashers until the base of the tin is covered.

Preheat the oven to 150°C/130°C fan/gas 2. Spoon the mixture into the lined terrine, pressing down into the edges of the dish. Bring the overlapping bacon up and over the mixture to cover the surface.

Cover with the lid (or foil) and place the terrine into a small roasting tin. Add enough just-boiled water to the roasting tin to come 2cm up the outside of the terrine. Bake in the centre of the oven for 1½ hours.

To test the terrine is ready, remove from the oven and insert a skewer into the centre. Hold for 10 seconds, then remove and lightly touch the end – the skewer should feel hot. The terrine should also have shrunk away from the sides of the dish. Remove from the roasting tin.

Take off the terrine lid, pierce the clingfilm and drain off the liquid released during cooking. Cover with a double layer of foil. Leave to cool, then put a heavy weight on top (such as a couple of cans of beans). Chill in the fridge overnight. The next day, turn the terrine out onto a board and cut into thick slices. Drizzle with olive oil, season with salt and pepper and scatter over the chopped pistachio nuts. Serve with sourdough bread and Onion Marmalade, and with the shallot and parsley scattered over.

Making a terrine

Crab with pear, chestnut and celeriac

This looks really great on the plate and it's nice and easy to prepare. For the best flavour, use homemade Mayonnaise (see page 272) to bind the celeriac and crab, but if you are using bought, I recommend you get a good-quality fresh one, as it makes all the difference to the end result. If fresh chestnuts are in season, please do try to use these; if not, the vacuum-packed ones make a good substitute.

Serves: 4–6 as a starter
Preparation time: 20 minutes

200g white crab meat
4 tbsp good-quality mayonnaise (or
    homemade Mayonnaise, page 272)
juice of 1 lemon
½ small celeriac
1 tsp wholegrain mustard
1 tsp chopped flat-leaf parsley leaves
1 ripe pear, cored and thinly sliced
2–4 fresh chestnuts, peeled, or 4–6
    pre-packed ones, shaved using a
    vegetable peeler or Microplane grater
sea salt and freshly ground black pepper

In a bowl, combine the crab meat with 2 tablespoons of the mayonnaise, half of the lemon juice and season with salt and black pepper. Set aside.

Peel the celeriac and cut into very fine strips, about the thickness of matchsticks. Put in a bowl and mix with the remaining mayonnaise and lemon juice, mustard, parsley and seasoning.

To serve, divide the crab between plates and spoon the celeriac to the side of the crab. Arrange the pear on top and finish with some chestnut shavings.

Tuna tartare with fennel, pickled ginger and soy dressing

There are a fair few elements to this recipe but they are all very easy to prepare. The main thing to point out here is you should try to buy the best-quality, 'sushi-grade' fresh tuna possible. If you are planning to make this for a dinner party and you have a fishmonger nearby, it's worth pre-ordering the tuna.

Serves: 4 as a starter
Preparation time: 1½ hours
Cooking time: 45 minutes

1 small fennel, very finely sliced (ideally
    on a mandoline)
juice of ½ lemon
300g sushi-grade fresh tuna
2 spring onions, finely shredded
shiso cress or salad cress, to serve
2 tsp toasted sesame seeds
sea salt, to season

FOR THE PICKLED GINGER
6cm piece of fresh ginger, peeled and
    very finely chopped
1 tbsp table salt
40g caster sugar
75ml rice wine/sushi vinegar

FOR THE DRESSING
15ml sesame oil
30ml soy sauce
15ml honey
15g caster sugar
1 tbsp lime juice
½ garlic clove, crushed
sea salt and freshly ground black pepper

To make the pickled ginger, sit the ginger in a sieve and sprinkle with the salt. Leave for 30 minutes and rinse.

Put the salted ginger in a saucepan with the sugar and vinegar. Stir over medium heat until the sugar dissolves. Bring to a simmer, loosely cover with a lid and leave to simmer very gently for 30 minutes. Remove from the heat and allow to cool.

Meanwhile, to make the dressing, vigorously whisk everything together until emulsified.

Toss the fennel in the lemon juice and season with salt and black pepper.

Dice the tuna into 1cm pieces. Strain the pickled ginger from the liquid and gently mix the ginger and tuna together along with 4 tablespoons of the soy dressing. Season.

To assemble, spoon the tuna onto plates and dress the rest of the plate with the fennel, spring onions and cress, then scatter over the sesame seeds. Serve with extra dressing separately, or store the dressing in an airtight jar in the fridge to use another day.

Marinated mackerel with crab, apple marmalade and smoked hazelnuts

You can really go to town with the assembly of this dish and give it a restaurant-style presentation. As we would in the restaurant, prepare all of the ingredients ahead so the assembly of the dish is quick and stress-free, but ensure that your mackerel is as fresh as possible.

Serves: 8 as a starter
Preparation time: 30 minutes
Cooking time: 15 minutes

10g butter
30g blanched hazelnuts
¼ tsp smoked paprika
2 tbsp olive oil
1 tsp white wine vinegar
6 skin-on mackerel fillets, pin-boned
  or v-cut
200g white crab meat
50g brown crab meat
Pink Lady apple, peeled and thinly sliced
coriander or salad cress, to serve
sea salt and freshly ground black pepper

FOR THE MARMALADE
75g caster sugar
115ml white wine vinegar
2 Braeburn apples

To make the marmalade, put the sugar and white wine vinegar into a saucepan and bring to the boil for 4 minutes. Meanwhile, peel, core and cut the apples into 4mm cubes. Add to the pan and simmer gently for 10 minutes. Pour into a shallow bowl and put in the fridge to cool.

Reduce the heat under the pan and add the butter. Once bubbling, toss in the hazelnuts and add the paprika. Move around in the pan until the hazelnuts are golden. Transfer to a bowl lined with kitchen paper to absorb any excess butter. Set aside to cool, then roughly chop.

Make a vinaigrette dressing by mixing the olive oil with 1 teaspoon of white wine vinegar. Season with salt and black pepper.

Remove the mackerel fillets from the fridge and cut in half lengthways, then in half horizontally. Coat the fillets in half of the vinaigrette and allow to marinate for 10 minutes. Season and mix the remaining vinaigrette with the white crab meat.

Divide the brown crabmeat between serving plates. Arrange the white crab, mackerel, apple marmalade and apple slices on top and scatter over the hazelnuts and coriander or salad cress to serve.

Tea-smoked vine tomato salad with pecorino

Smoking tomatoes over tea gives them a really unique flavour, but you must use ripe, rich red tomatoes for this recipe to achieve their full effect in this fabulous salad.

Serves: 4 as a starter
Preparation time: 15 minutes
Smoking time: 40 minutes

150g sea salt
150g uncooked rice
25g lapsang souchong tea leaves
500g small ripe tomatoes, about the size of golf balls
60ml extra virgin olive oil, plus extra for drizzling
¼ bunch of thyme, leaves picked and chopped
2 sprigs of rosemary, leaves picked and finely chopped
1 tsp rock salt
½ tsp freshly ground black pepper
½ tsp smoked paprika
150g piece of pecorino cheese
shiso cress, to serve

Line a heavy-based baking tray or flameproof baking dish with foil and scatter over the salt, rice and tea. Sit a wire rack on top, one that sits inside the baking tray, making sure the bottom of the rack doesn't touch the rice.

Cut the tomatoes in half and toss them in a bowl with the oil, herbs, rock salt, pepper and paprika. Sit the tomatoes on the wire rack, cut-side facing up.

Cover the entire wire rack and tray with foil, making sure no smoke will escape.

Put the tray over medium heat and leave to smoke for 10 minutes. Remove from the heat and leave the foil in place for 30 minutes.

Arrange the smoked tomatoes on serving plates, drizzle with extra virgin olive oil, sprinkle with the cress and shave over shards of pecorino.

Roast chicken with herb, pistachio and sourdough citrus stuffing

This may be more labour intensive than the Sunday Roast Chicken (see page 100), but it's more than worth it if you've got the time. Not only does this look impressive when carved into, it tastes out of this world, too.

Serves: 4–6
Preparation time: 1 hour
Cooking time: 1 hour 20 minutes, plus
　　resting

1 large chicken
4 bay leaves
½ lemon (use the stuffing zested lemon)
½ orange (use the stuffing zested orange)
1 garlic bulb, halved
olive oil, for drizzling
100ml white wine or sherry
750ml Chicken Stock (page 270)
2 tbsp cornflour (optional)
sea salt and freshly ground black pepper

FOR THE STUFFING
50g butter
1 small onion, finely chopped
1 celery stick, finely chopped
2 garlic cloves, finely chopped
150g sourdough, crusts removed
150g pistachio nuts
finely grated zest of ½ lemon
finely grated zest of ½ orange
1 tsp celery salt
1 tsp freshly ground black pepper
1 egg, beaten
½ bunch of tarragon, leaves finely chopped
½ bunch of flat-leaf parsley, leaves finely
　　chopped
½ bunch of coriander, leaves finely
　　chopped

To make the stuffing, melt the butter in a frying pan over medium heat. Add the onion, celery and garlic and cook until softened but not coloured. Transfer to a large bowl to cool.

Put the sourdough in a food processor and blitz until you have fine crumbs. Add to the bowl with the cooled onions. Blitz the pistachios until finely chopped and mix into the bowl with the lemon and orange zests, celery salt, pepper, egg and herbs.

Slide your fingers between the chicken skin and breast flesh to create pockets. Press the stuffing under the skin, pressing and moving so that the mixture covers as much of the breast as possible. Stuff the rest into the neck end of the chicken and secure with a cocktail stick or two.

Preheat the oven to 200°C/180°C fan/gas 6.

Put the chicken in a roasting tray and stuff the bay leaves, lemon, orange and garlic into the bird's cavity. Drizzle with oil and season well. Cook for 1 hour and 20 minutes, until the outside is golden. Test the chicken is cooked by inserting a skewer into the fattest part of the thigh, if the juices run clear it is done. Carefully remove the chicken from the tray (pour any juices from the cavity back into the tray), place on a board to rest for 10–15 minutes, covered loosely with foil.

Put the roasting tray over high heat, add the white wine and stir with a wooden spoon to deglaze, loosening and incorporating any sediment from the bottom of the tray. Add the chicken stock and boil until the liquid has reduced to about 600ml. If you prefer a thicker sauce, mix the cornflour with 2 tablespoons of cold water to form a paste, and add this to the pan. Boil for a couple of minutes, whisking until thickened. Add a little more seasoning, if you like, and pour into a jug.

Carve the chicken and spoon the stuffing from inside the neck and serve with gravy.

Poached and marinated chicken, carrot purée and pickle

Don't let the length of this recipe stop you giving this one a go. It's all very straightforward and the final flavours are fresh, light and aromatic.

Serves: 2 or 4 as a starter
Preparation time: 45 minutes, plus overnight pickling and 2 hours marinating
Cooking time: 25 minutes

FOR THE POACHED CHICKEN
750ml Chicken Stock (page 270)
2 shallots, roughly chopped
4 garlic cloves, smashed
2 star anise
1 tsp fennel seeds
2 large skin-on chicken breasts

FOR THE CHICKEN MARINADE
1 tsp fennel seeds, lightly toasted in a frying pan
2 star anise, lightly crushed
2 sprigs of thyme
pinch of salt
150ml olive oil, plus extra if needed

FOR THE CARROT PICKLE
150g purple carrots
2 garlic cloves
1 tbsp extra virgin olive oil
1 tsp celery salt
2 tsp yellow mustard seeds
50ml white wine vinegar

FOR THE CARROT PURÉE
30g butter
300g carrots, coarsely grated
pinch of sea salt
1 tbsp olive oil
sea salt and freshly ground black pepper

coriander cress or salad cress, to serve
2–3 rainbow carrots (purple, yellow and orange), sliced into ribbons and put in iced water to curl, to serve

To make the carrot pickle, very thinly slice the purple carrots and garlic, ideally using a mandoline, and mix with the remaining pickle ingredients and 50ml of water. Cover and leave overnight to pickle.

For the chicken, put the stock, shallots, garlic, star anise and fennel seeds in a saucepan and bring to a rolling boil. Reduce to a simmer and add the chicken for 8 minutes. Remove from the heat and leave to continue cooking in the hot stock for 5 minutes.

Remove the chicken from the stock and put in a bowl along with all of the marinade ingredients, making sure the chicken is covered in the oil, adding extra if needed. Cover with clingfilm and put in the fridge to marinate for around 2 hours, though longer is fine.

Meanwhile, to make the carrot purée, melt the butter in a saucepan and add the carrots, 2 tablespoons of water and salt. Stir around in the pan for a couple of minutes until the carrots start to soften. Cover with a lid and cook for 8–10 minutes, stirring occasionally until the carrots are completely soft. Transfer to a blender and blitz to a smooth purée along with the oil. Taste and add more seasoning, if you like.

To finish the chicken, place a frying pan over high heat. Remove the chicken from the marinade and shake off any spice or herbs. Cut both breasts in half, giving you 4 smaller portions. Put skin-side down into the pan and leave for 3–4 minutes to crisp up the skin and lightly warm the chicken through.

To assemble the dish, spoon some carrot purée onto the centre of your serving plates. Sit the chicken on top and spoon the carrot pickle to the side. Serve with curls of rainbow carrot ribbons and scatter some cress over the top.

Confit duck leg with borlotti, chorizo and sage

Forget quick cooking here, this is all about taking it slow. The duck legs are first salted/cured for 4 hours to completely change their texture and flavour, then they are very gently cooked in duck fat and herbs. Cook them too quickly and their wonderful texture will be spoiled, but don't rush it and the result will be meltingly tender meat that falls off the bone. *(See image on following pages.)*

Serves: 4
Preparation time: 20 minutes, plus
    4 hours salting
Cooking time: 4 hours 15 minutes to
    5 hours 15 minutes

4 skin-on duck legs
250g rock salt
800g duck fat
¼ bunch of thyme
2 bay leaves

FOR THE BORLOTTI, CHORIZO
    AND SAGE
2 tbsp olive oil
1 small celeriac, diced into 1cm cubes
1 × 400g tin borlotti beans, drained
1 bunch of sage, leaves picked and finely
    chopped
200g Chorizo Jam (page 274)
100g baby spinach leaves
salt and black pepper

Lay the duck legs, skin-side up, in a shallow bowl or tray. Sprinkle over the rock salt and leave in the fridge for about 4 hours.

Rinse the salt from the duck legs and pat dry.

Preheat the oven to 150°C/130°C fan/gas 2.

Heat the duck fat in a medium-sized roasting tray over medium heat, until melted. Add the thyme, bay leaves and duck, skin-side down, ensuring the duck is covered in the fat. If not, add some more duck fat. Cover with foil and slowly cook for 4–5 hours until the duck is tender. Cool slightly, then carefully remove from the fat.

Increase the oven temperature to 220°C/200°C fan/gas 6.

Put a large pan over medium heat and add the olive oil. When hot, put in the diced celeriac and sauté for 8–10 minutes until tender.

Put the duck in a clean roasting tray and roast, skin-side up, for 10 minutes. If the skin isn't crisp enough, finish it off under the grill.

Add the borlotti beans, sage leaves and chorizo jam to the celeriac. Stir until everything is heated through. Finish by stirring through the spinach, add more seasoning, if you like, and serve with the duck.

Rack of lamb with fennel, anchovy, black olive and goat's cheese salad

Ask your butcher for some lamb bones to make this vinaigrette – it is well worth the effort. If, however, this isn't an option, then I recommend you buy some separate lamb chops and cut off the bones. Pop the meat in the freezer to use for a quick-cook recipe another day and use the bones for the vinaigrette.

Serves: 4
Preparation time: 45 minutes, plus
    24–48 hours marinating
Cooking time: up to 2½ hours

2 French-trimmed lamb racks, each with
    6 bones (3 per person), cut into chops
150ml olive oil
3 sprigs of rosemary
3 sprigs of thyme
2 tbsp vegetable oil
sea salt and freshly ground black pepper

FOR THE VINAIGRETTE
250g lamb bones
1 garlic bulb, halved
1 celery stick, halved
1 carrot, halved
200ml white wine
3 sprigs of rosemary
2 bay leaves
750ml Chicken or Vegetable Stock (pages
    270–1)
125ml extra virgin olive oil
25ml good-quality sherry vinegar

FOR THE SALAD
2 tbsp extra virgin olive oil
1 tsp lemon juice
50g anchovy fillets, cut to 1cm pieces
50g pitted kalamata olives, sliced into
    strips
1 medium-large fennel, very finely sliced
    (ideally on a mandoline)
120g soft goat's cheese

Put the lamb chops in a bowl or strong freezer bag and pour over the olive oil. Add the rosemary and thyme sprigs and leave to marinate for 24–28 hours, turning the lamb around every so often.

To make the lamb vinaigrette, preheat the oven to 220°C/200°C fan/gas 7. Put the lamb bones in a small roasting tray with the garlic and roast for 30–40 minutes, until deep golden. Add the celery and carrot and continue to roast for a further 10 minutes.

Pour in the wine and return to the oven for around 10 minutes or until the wine has evaporated to a syrupy consistency. Add the rosemary sprigs, bay leaves and stock. Reduce the oven to 180°C/160°C fan/gas 4. Cook for 1 hour, then remove from the oven, leaving the oven on.

Strain the roasting liquid into a saucepan and bring to the boil over high heat until thickened. Allow to cool, then stir in the olive oil and sherry vinegar, and season to taste. Set aside.

To cook the lamb chops, heat the vegetable oil in a griddle pan on high heat. Remove the lamb from the marinade and season with salt and black pepper. Add to the pan and grill well on each side. Put in the oven and cook for a further 5–10 minutes. Depending on how you like your lamb cooked, 5 minutes will give you rare and 10 minutes medium-well done. Remove from the oven and leave to rest for the same amount of time that you cooked the lamb in the oven.

For the salad, mix together the oil, lemon juice, anchovies and olives. Add the fennel and toss together.

To assemble, spoon the salad onto plates and crumble over a generous spoonful of goat's cheese. Arrange the chops on the plates. Spoon over the vinaigrette and serve straight away.

Rare roast beef salad with asparagus and yuzu

This is a wonderfully fresh main course in spring, when asparagus is in season. Yuzu is an aromatic Asian citrus fruit that tastes like a combination of grapefruit, mandarin and lemon.

Serves: 4–6
Preparation time: 35–40 minutes
Cooking time: 20–25 minutes

1 tbsp vegetable oil
750g sirloin
sea salt and freshly ground black pepper

FOR THE VINAIGRETTE
200ml Beef Stock (page 270)
1 tbsp red wine vinegar
50ml sesame oil
50ml olive oil
½ tsp wasabi

FOR THE MAYONNAISE
1 egg yolk
¼ tsp English mustard
½ tbsp honey
50ml olive oil
125ml vegetable oil
25ml yuzu juice

FOR THE ASPARAGUS
1 bunch of asparagus, woody ends
   trimmed, cut in half
250ml vegetable oil
2 banana shallots
2 tbsp flour
¼ bunch of tarragon, leaves picked
¼ bunch of coriander, leaves picked
¼ bunch of parsley, leaves picked
200g baby salad leaves

FOR THE YUZU DRESSING
50ml olive oil
10ml yuzu juice
1 tsp honey

Preheat the oven to 120°C/100°C fan/gas ½. Heat a large frying pan with the oil and season the sirloin. When the oil is smoking, sear the sirloin on all sides until golden. Place in a roasting dish and into the oven for 15–20 minutes until a core temperature of 40°C is reached. Remove and cool. Place in the fridge.

For the vinaigrette, bring the stock to the boil and reduce until 50ml is left. Whisk in all the other ingredients and set aside.

For the mayonnaise, whisk the yolk until fluffy, add the mustard and honey, then slowly add the oils. Whisk until thick, then let down with the yuzu juice and season to taste.

Bring a large pan of salted water to the boil. Blanch the asparagus for 90 seconds until tender, then refresh in iced water until cool. Drain well.

Heat the oil in a small pan, or in your deep fryer, until hot. Slice the shallots, forming rings, poking out the centre piece and discarding. Separate the rings using your hands, then coat in flour. Deep-fry until crispy, season well, and set aside on absorbent paper.

For the yuzu vinaigrette, whisk together the oil, yuzu juice and honey. Mix the picked herbs with the salad leaves in a bowl, toss with the yuzu dressing and season well.

Slice the beef into thin slices and lay on a tray. Dress with the beef vinaigrette and season very well. Place the beef onto 4–6 plates.

Dress and season the asparagus and salad leaves with the yuzu vinaigrette, and place these alongside the beef. Dress with the yuzu mayonnaise and shallot rings.

Braised oxtail ravioli

Gyoza or wonton wrappers are available from Chinese/Asian supermarkets or online. They make an ideal case for these ravioli, and are far easier to use than fresh pasta. As for the stock, do use fresh if possible (see page 270). If making your own isn't an option, you can buy good-quality tubs, which are ideal. The recipe makes plenty of sauce, and any left over can be frozen and used as an exceptionally tasty gravy.

Serves: 4
Preparation time: 30 minutes
Cooking time: 3 hours 30 minutes

3 tbsp plain flour
1kg oxtail, sliced
2 tbsp vegetable oil
1 garlic bulb, halved
few sprigs of rosemary
few sprigs of thyme
2 bay leaves
1 onion, quartered
3 carrots, quartered
1 leek, white part only, roughly chopped
2 celery sticks, roughly chopped
500ml red wine
250ml port
2 tbsp tomato purée
3 tbsp black treacle
5 white peppercorns
1 star anise
750ml veal or Beef Stock, preferably homemade or good-quality shop-bought (page 270)
750ml Chicken Stock, preferably home-made or good-quality shop-bought (page 270)
2 tbsp sherry vinegar
3 tbsp chopped flat-leaf parsley leaves
20g unsalted butter
1 small celeriac, diced into ½–1cm pieces
36 gyoza wrappers (1½ packets, approx. 210g, available from Asian supermarkets)
sea salt and freshly ground black pepper
olive oil, for drizzling

Season the flour with salt and pepper and toss the oxtail in it. Heat the oil in a large casserole dish. Once smoking hot, brown the oxtail all over, then remove from the pan. Add the garlic, herbs and vegetables to the pan and cook for 10–15 minutes, until golden. Add the wine, port and tomato purée and cook over high heat until reduced to a syrupy consistency.

Return the oxtail to the pan with the treacle, peppercorns, star anise and both stocks. Bring to a very gentle simmer, cover and cook for 3 hours, or until the meat is falling off the bone.

Strain the sauce into a clean saucepan, then bring it to a simmer over moderate heat and cook until reduced by half. Pick the meat from the bones into a bowl. Add enough of the reduced sauce to loosely bind the meat together, then mix in the sherry vinegar, 1 tablespoon of the flat-leaf parsley and check for seasoning. Reserve the remaining sauce for serving.

Melt the butter in a saucepan over medium heat until foaming. Add the celeriac and a good pinch of salt and cook for about 5 minutes until the celeriac is golden and tender. Add to the oxtail mixture.

To make the ravioli, brush the outside edges of one of the gyoza wrappers with water. Place a small spoonful of the oxtail filling in the centre and place another gyoza wrapper on top. Press the edges to seal, making sure you remove any air trapped inside. Continue with the remaining wrappers and filling until you have 18 ravioli. Arrange them in a single layer in a steamer set over a pan of boiling water (you may need to work in batches, keeping the cooked dumplings hot while you cook the rest). Steam for 5 minutes.

Heat the reserved sauce and serve with the ravioli and drizzle with olive oil.

Venison, squash purée and beetroot granola

This is a simplified version of one of my very popular restaurant dishes. The rich sauce, tender venison and sweet squash purée are perfectly paired with the crunchy, nutty granola. This is perfect comfort food, made into an impressive dish for entertaining.

Serves: 6
Preparation time: 45 minutes
Cooking time: 2 hours

4 tbsp vegetable oil
2 celery stalks, quartered
1 leek, white part only, quartered
1 carrot, quartered
2 bay leaves
2 star anise
10 juniper berries
4 cloves
200ml port
200ml red wine
2 tbsp red wine vinegar
2 tbsp black treacle
500ml veal or Beef Stock (page 270)
500ml Chicken Stock (page 270)
6 loin of venison portions
sea salt and freshly ground black pepper

FOR THE GRANOLA
100g oats
20g pumpkin seeds
25g sunflower seeds
50g pecan nuts, chopped
50g dried cranberries, roughly chopped
100g cooked beetroot
100g honey
2 tsp thyme leaves

FOR THE PURÉE
1 tbsp vegetable oil
1 medium-large butternut squash, cut into 3cm thick pieces
4 sprigs of rosemary
50g butter

Heat a large ovenproof casserole over high heat and add half the oil, the celery, leek and carrot to the pan and lightly brown. Stir in the bay leaves and spices, then pour in the port, red wine and vinegar. Bring to the boil and reduce the liquid by about a third.

Add the treacle and stocks. Return to the boil, then reduce the liquid to a thick, syrupy consistency. Strain through a sieve, season with salt and pepper and keep hot.

Preheat the oven to 160°C/140°C fan/gas 3. For the beetroot granola put the oats, seeds, pecan nuts and cranberries in a mixing bowl and stir together. Put the beetroot, honey and thyme in a blender and blitz to a smooth purée. Mix into the dried oat mixture and tip onto a non-stick baking sheet. Bake in the oven for 20–30 minutes until golden and crisp, turning on the tray a few times to ensure it cooks evenly. Remove and leave to cool.

To make the squash purée, heat the oil in a roasting tray over medium heat, add the squash and fry until slightly coloured. Season with salt and pepper and add the rosemary. Place in the oven for about 30 minutes, until the squash is tender.

Melt the butter in a small saucepan over medium heat. Increase the heat and allow the butter to become a nutty brown in colour.

Transfer the soft squash to a blender, add the browned butter and blitz until smooth. Season and keep hot.

Heat the remaining oil in a non-stick pan over high heat. Season the venison and brown in the pan on all sides. Finish off in the oven for 10 minutes. Rest for 5 minutes, then slice. Serve the squash purée with the venison on top and the beetroot granola and reduced sauce.

Prawn orzo risotto with monkfish

If you've not made a risotto with orzo before, now's your chance. The small rice-shaped pasta is an ideal dinner-party ingredient, as unlike traditional risotto rice you don't have to stand and constantly stir it while it cooks. Just treat it like standard pasta and cook until al dente in boiling salted water, then drain and add the risotto ingredients just before you plan to serve.

This particular recipe has a fair amount of advance preparation, but the end result is quite simply exceptional. First there's a rich and decadent prawn bisque to make, which creates the base flavour to the risotto (it's also delicious on its own and can also be used as a sauce accompaniment to any fish dish). Then there's the delicious prawn butter that you stir through the risotto at the end, which really enriches it. The butter is also used to gently cook the monkfish, creating a delicious, full-flavoured dish.

Both the bisque and Prawn Butter (page 276) use just the shells of the prawns, which leaves you with plenty of uncooked peeled prawns. I love to use these for the Prawns with Prawn Butter, Sweetcorn and Cornbread (see page 138), or you can simply pop them in the freezer to use another day.

Serves: 4
Preparation time: 25 minutes
Cooking time: approx. 1 hour
   15 minutes

300g orzo pasta
100g mascarpone
½ tsp smoked paprika
2 tbsp chopped tarragon
4 monkfish tail portions
1 tbsp vegetable oil
50g Prawn Butter (page 276)
sea salt and freshly ground black pepper

To make the bisque, heat 1 tablespoon of the oil in a large saucepan over high heat until it is smoking. Add the prawn shells and cook until they are dark golden. Remove from the pan and set aside.

Add the remaining oil to the pan and then add the onion, celery, carrot, garlic, leek, fennel, coriander seeds, fennel seeds and peppercorns. Cook until the vegetables are dark golden. Stir in the tomato purée, brandy and white wine. Boil until you have a syrupy consistency.

Return the prawn shells to the pan along with the thyme, tarragon, bay leaves, chicken stock and 1 litre of water. Bring to a simmer and cook for 30 minutes.

FOR THE BISQUE
2 tbsp vegetable oil
shells from 1kg prawns
½ onion, chopped
1 celery stalk, chopped
1 carrot, chopped
2 garlic cloves
½ small leek, white part only, chopped
½ fennel bulb, sliced
½ tsp coriander seeds
½ tsp fennel seeds
5 white peppercorns
50g tomato purée
125ml brandy
350ml white wine
few sprigs of thyme
few sprigs of tarragon
2 bay leaves
1 litre Chicken Stock (page 270)
1 tbsp Pernod
200ml double cream
sea salt

Strain the bisque through a sieve into a clean pan, pushing all of the liquid through by pressing with the base of a ladle. Return to a simmer and reduce in quantity by half. Season with salt, stir in the Pernod and cream. Return to a simmer, then the bisque is ready to use or keep chilled for 2 days.

To make the risotto, cook the orzo in boiling salted water as per the packet instructions until almost cooked. Drain.

Put the cooked orzo in a saucepan and place over medium-low heat. Stir in 300ml of the prawn bisque and heat through. Add the mascarpone, smoked paprika and tarragon. Stir until the mascarpone has melted and is piping hot.

Meanwhile, cook the monkfish. Heat the oil in a medium-large frying pan over medium-high heat. Season the monkfish with salt and black pepper, then add to the pan to lightly brown all over. Add half of the prawn butter and continue cooking, using a spoon to baste the monkfish with the butter for about 5 minutes.

Finish the orzo by adding the remaining prawn butter, then add more seasoning, if you like. Spoon into pasta bowls and sit the monkfish on top.

Sea bass with girolles, kabocha squash and pumpkin seeds

Kabocha squash is very sweet and has a green (sometimes orange) skin and a bright orange flesh that has a fluffy chestnut texture similar to a sweet potato crossed with a pumpkin. This vegetable is used widely in Asia and is becoming more easily available here – in season from late summer through to autumn.

Serves: 4
Preparation time: 20 minutes
Cooking time: 30 minutes

125g butter
1 kabocha squash, deseeded and halved
100ml milk
2 sprigs of rosemary
100ml Vegetable Stock (page 271)
2 tbsp maple syrup
50g toasted pumpkin seeds, roughly chopped
2 tbsp olive oil
4 skin-on sea bass fillets, scaled, pin-boned and skin scored
200g girolle mushrooms, cleaned
½ tsp sea salt, plus extra for seasoning
micro coriander, to serve

Melt 50g butter in a saucepan over medium heat. Cut one half of the squash into chunks and add to the butter. Fry until the squash begins to soften, then add the milk and rosemary and season well with salt. Bring to a simmer and cook for 10–15 minutes, until the squash is completely soft. Transfer to a blender and blitz to a smooth purée. Return to the pan and keep warm.

Heat a further 50g butter in a large frying pan over medium-high heat. Cut the remaining squash into 12 wedges and fry on both sides until lightly golden. Pour over the stock and cook for 6–8 minutes, until no stock remains in the pan, turning the wedges a couple of times. Remove the rosemary, pour the maple syrup over the squash and turn to glaze on both sides. Sprinkle over the pumpkin seeds and keep hot.

For the sea bass, heat a large non-stick frying pan over high heat. Add the oil, season the sea bass with salt and sit skin-side down in the pan. Cook without moving for 4 minutes, until the skin is crispy. Carefully turn over and cook for a further minute. If you don't have a pan large enough, do this in two batches.

Remove the fish from the pan. Wipe out the pan with kitchen paper and return to the heat. Add the remaining butter and when it's foaming, add the mushrooms and ½ teaspoon salt, and fry for a few minutes.

To assemble, place a spoonful of the squash purée on the base of the plates and top with the mushrooms and squash wedges. Finish with the sea bass, scatter over the micro coriander and serve straight away.

Salmon, fennel, bouillabaisse and rouille

This dish is a take on a classic fish soup but uses salmon instead of white fish and shellfish. It comprises three elements, all coming together to create a superb dinner party dish that will go down a treat with your guests.

It's very easy to overcook salmon, making it dry and firm textured, but when quickly pan-fried then slowly finished off in a low oven the result is evenly cooked, incredibly juicy, melt-in-the-mouth fish. You can use this cooking method for all sorts of salmon recipes, not just this one, and cooking it this way makes it virtually impossible to overcook the fillets.

If you are lucky enough to have a local fishmonger, ask them for some fish bones, minus heads, to make the bouillabaisse here. You may find the fishmongers in the supermarket will give you them – it's less waste for them to deal with.

The final part to the recipe is the rouille, which is a classic Provençal sauce served as a garnish with bouillabaisse. Traditionally breadcrumbs are used to thicken the garlic and olive oil, but here I am using potato, which gives a smoother finish.

Serves: 6
Preparation time: 45 minutes
Cooking time: 1 hour 30 minutes

6 thick skinless salmon fillets
2 tbsp vegetable oil, plus extra
1 large fennel, finely sliced with a
    mandoline
squeeze of lemon juice
sea salt and freshly ground black pepper

To make the bouillabaisse, heat 1 tablespoon of oil in a large saucepan and add the fish bones. Cook for a few minutes until they are browned. Remove from the pan and set aside.

Add the remaining 1 tablespoon of oil and fry the onion, fennel, carrot, leek, celery, garlic, star anise and saffron, until browned.

Stir in the tomatoes and tomato purée. Cook for a minute, then add the wine and Pernod. Boil until the liquid has reduced down completely.

Return the fish bones to the pan, pour in 1.5 litres of water and add a good pinch of salt and paprika. Bring to a simmer and cook for 1 hour.

To make the rouille, put the potato and garlic in a pan of salted water and bring to the boil. Cook for 15–20 minutes until tender. Drain well and mash until smooth.

FOR THE BOUILLABAISSE

2 tbsp olive oil
1kg fish bones (no heads), roughly
  chopped
1 small onion, chopped
1 small fennel, chopped
1 small carrot, chopped
½ leek, white part only, chopped
1 celery stick, chopped
4 garlic cloves, peeled
1 star anise
pinch of saffron
3 plum tomatoes, roughly chopped
1 tbsp tomato purée
250ml white wine
50ml Pernod
pinch of sea salt
½ tsp smoked paprika

FOR THE ROUILLE

1 potato, halved
1 garlic clove
25g piquillo peppers
pinch of saffron
2 egg yolks
¼ red chilli, deseeded and chopped
grated zest of ¼ lemon
200ml olive oil

Put the piquillo peppers, saffron, egg yolks, chilli and lemon zest in a blender and blitz until smooth. Gradually add the olive oil until well combined. Finish by adding the potato and briefly blitzing to combine, giving you a thick, mayonnaise-like consistency. Season to taste and set aside.

To cook the salmon, preheat the oven to 120°C/100°C fan/ gas 1. Heat a non-stick frying pan with the oil. When hot, season the salmon on both sides. Sear in batches of three, for 3 minutes on each side. Place in a baking dish and bake for 8–12 minutes until just cooked through.

To finish the bouillabaisse, blend well, in batches, in a food processor, then pass through a sieve, pressing down with the base of a ladle to extract as much of the liquid and flavour as possible. Season to taste.

Serve the salmon with some of the bouillabaisse spooned over the top. Toss the fennel in a little olive oil, lemon juice and salt, pile on top of the salmon and finish with some rouille.

Brill with mussels, samphire and parsley pappardelle

Brill is a flat fish with a sweet taste and firm texture that lends itself really well to poaching in this light, buttery liquor.

Serves: 4
Preparation time: 30 minutes
Cooking time: 25 minutes

50g unsalted butter
2 banana shallots, finely chopped
zest and juice of ½ lemon
4 skin-on brill fillets
100ml white wine
20 cockles, cleaned
20 mussels, cleaned
100g samphire
25ml white vermouth
sea salt and freshly ground black pepper

FOR THE PAPPARDELLE
60g soft butter
½ bunch flat-leaf parsley, roughly
    chopped
½ tsp garlic salt
350g dried egg pappardelle pasta

For the pappardelle, put the butter, parsley and garlic salt in a small food processor and blend to give a green-flecked butter. Alternatively, finely chop the parsley and mix with the butter and garlic salt.

Cook the pasta in a pan of boiling salted water for the time stated on the packet. Drain and immediately toss with the butter to coat. Keep hot.

For the brill, add half of the butter to a large frying pan over medium-high heat. Add the shallots and sauté until softened and slightly golden. Finish with the lemon zest and a little juice.

Season the brill and put in with the shallots, skin-side up. Cook for 30 seconds before adding the white wine. Turn the fish over and add the cockles and mussels to the pan. Cover with a lid, reduce the heat and gently poach for a few minutes until the shells open, discarding any that remain closed.

Add the remaining butter to the brill and gently swirl and stir the pan to create an emulsion around the fish. Add the samphire, coating in the sauce and cook for a few minutes. Season by adding a squeeze of lemon juice, some vermouth and salt.

Remove the skin from the brill, then divide among four plates. Spoon over the parsley pappardelle and finish with mussels, samphire and sauce.

Butternut squash and sage dumplings with hazelnut and coconut sauce and kale

I use gyoza or wonton wrappers a lot as a handy alternative to fresh pasta when making ravioli. Here they're stuffed with a classic Italian ravioli filling, but to mix things up they contain a fusion of flavours that work amazingly well together.
(See step-by-step technique on following pages.)

Serves: 6
Preparation time: 30 minutes
Cooking time: 50 minutes

approx. 30 gyoza wrappers
200g kale, tough stalks removed
1 tbsp coconut oil
2 tbsp roughly chopped roasted
    hazelnuts, to serve

FOR THE FILLING
350g diced butternut squash
180g ricotta cheese
½ nutmeg, freshly grated
2 tbsp chopped sage

FOR THE SAUCE
1cm piece of fresh ginger, peeled and
    finely chopped
50g blanched hazelnuts, chopped
400ml coconut milk
2 tbsp sweet sherry
¼ nutmeg, freshly grated, plus extra to
    serve
sea salt and freshly ground black pepper

For the dumpling filling, arrange the squash in a steamer set over simmering water and steam for 8–10 minutes, until tender. Allow to cool, then put in a blender or food processor with the ricotta, nutmeg, sage and seasoning. Pulse-blend until combined but be careful not to over-mix.

To make the sauce, put the ginger and hazelnuts in a small saucepan and lightly toast. Add the remaining sauce ingredients and bring to a simmer. Cover and simmer for 20 minutes, then use a stick blender to blitz until smooth. Season to taste with salt and black pepper.

Lay 3–4 gyoza wrappers on the worktop and brush the outside edges with water. Place a heaped teaspoonful of the filling onto each wrapper, fold on the diagonal and pinch the edges together to make a triangle shape. Repeat with the remaining filling and wrappers.

Arrange the dumplings in a single layer in a steamer set over simmering water. Steam for 10–12 minutes before serving.

For the kale, lightly steam until just tender, then heat the coconut oil in a large frying pan or wok. When really hot, add the kale and toss until lightly golden on the edges. Season with salt and black pepper and divide between plates or bowls. Sit the dumplings on top and finish by spooning over the sauce and garnishing with chopped hazelnuts and freshly grated nutmeg.

Making dumplings

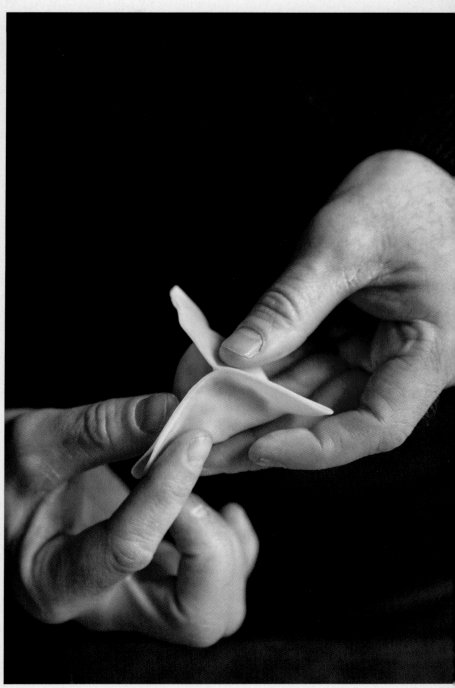

Forest mushroom fritters with mushroom fricassee

I like to cook these forest mushroom fritters in individual blini pans (small frying pans). If you don't have one, you can use a large frying pan and shape them into neat circles in the pan with a 10cm pastry cutter. They make a great vegetarian main course.

Serves: 4
Preparation time: 30 minutes
Cooking time: 1 hour

100g spelt
1 tsp cumin seeds
2 tbsp vegetable oil, plus extra for frying
2 banana shallots, finely chopped
300g flat mushrooms, diced
2 garlic cloves, crushed
2 tbsp chopped flat-leaf parsley leaves
50g Cheddar cheese, grated
30g plain flour
1 tsp wholegrain mustard
25g butter
sea salt and freshly ground black pepper

FOR THE FRICASSEE
1 tbsp vegetable oil
300g mixed mushrooms (try a selection such as chestnut, button or wild), sliced
2 tbsp Madeira wine
75ml double cream
1 tsp sherry vinegar
1 tbsp chopped flat-leaf parsley leaves
salad cress, to serve

To make the fritters, cook the spelt in a pan of boiling salted water for 20 minutes, until tender, or cook according to the packet instructions. Drain and set side.

Heat a large frying pan over medium heat and toast the cumin seeds for about 1 minute until they release their spicy aroma. Tip into a mixing bowl.

Return the pan to the heat and add the oil. When hot, add the shallots and sauté until they are starting to soften without taking on any colour. Add the diced flat mushrooms and garlic. Cook over medium-high heat until the mushrooms are golden and all of their moisture has evaporated.

Add the shallots and mushrooms to the cumin seeds. Mix in the parsley, Cheddar, flour, mustard and cooked spelt. Season with salt and pepper.

Divide the mixture into four. Heat small blini pans over medium heat and add a piece of butter and a drop of oil to each one. When the butter is frothing, add the fritter mixture and fry for about 3 minutes each side, carefully turning over with a spatula, until each side is golden.

For the fricassee, heat a large frying pan over high heat and add the oil. Add the mixed mushrooms and a pinch of salt. Fry until golden. Add the Madeira and cook until it has evaporated, before adding the cream, vinegar and parsley. Stir for about 1 minute, then season with salt and black pepper.

Sit the fritters on plates, spoon over the mushroom fricassee and scatter with salad cress.

Yuzu and maple parfait with rosemary shortbread

Citrusy and aromatic yuzu juice, sweet maple syrup and rich double cream are a surprisingly good combination and make a very refreshing dessert. I should point out that you will need a sugar thermometer here, which is a handy piece of kitchen kit to invest in if you've not already got one.

Serves: 6–8
Preparation time: 30 minutes plus at
   least 3 hours freezing

225ml maple syrup
2 sheets of gelatine
6 egg yolks
450ml double cream
50ml yuzu juice
lemon curd, to serve

FOR THE ROSEMARY SHORTBREAD
120g plain flour
70g cornflour
70g icing sugar, sifted
½ tsp sea salt
10g rosemary, finely chopped
120g diced butter, cold

FOR THE ROSEMARY SUGAR
15g caster sugar
1 sprig of rosemary

Put the maple syrup in a small saucepan and bring to the boil. Meanwhile, soak the gelatine in a bowl of cold water to soften and line a large loaf tin with clingfilm.

Put the egg yolks in a bowl and set over a pan of simmering water (making sure the bowl does not touch the water). Pour over the just-boiled maple syrup and beat with an electric hand whisk until you have a really thick and creamy mixture that holds ribbon shapes when the whisk is lifted.

Squeeze the excess water from the gelatine and drop one sheet at a time into the mixture, whisking as it dissolves. Remove the bowl from the heat and continue to whisk for up to 10 minutes until the mixture has cooled.

Put the cream and yuzu juice in a bowl, whisk until starting to thicken, then fold into the egg mixture until smooth. Transfer to the prepared loaf tin (or for individual parfaits you can set in round or square moulds) and put in the freezer for at least 3 hours to firm up.

To make the shortbread, put all of the dry ingredients and rosemary into a food processor and blitz to combine. Add the butter and pulse-blend until you have a dough. It may take some time for the butter to work into the dry ingredients. Tip onto the worktop and lightly knead until you have a velvety smooth dough. Roll out to about 1cm thick and press into the greased baking tin, pressing into the edges. Bake for 35–40 minutes until golden and firm.

While the shortbread is cooking, rub the sugar and rosemary stalk together to infuse the sugar. When the shortbread comes out of the oven, dust the rosemary sugar over the top. Cut into pieces in the tin while warm.

When ready to serve, remove from the freezer and run a hot knife around the edge of the tin. Slice into portions and serve with the shortbread and a dollop of lemon curd.

Caramelised white chocolate mousse cake

I absolutely love this recipe and it always goes down very well. To caramelise the white chocolate it needs to be baked until it becomes dark and crumbly; this may seem a little unusual but the flavour it produces works so well.

Serves: 8–12
Preparation time: 45 minutes, plus
    4 hours 40 minutes chilling
Cooking time: 40 minutes

FOR THE CHOCOLATE BASE
groundnut or vegetable oil, for greasing
50g butter, diced
75g icing sugar, sifted
pinch of salt
1 egg
180g strong white bread flour, plus extra
    for rolling
15g cocoa powder, sifted

FOR THE FILLING
325g white chocolate, broken into pieces
3 gelatine leaves
100ml milk
400ml whipping cream
seeds from 1 vanilla pod
3 egg yolks
40g caster sugar

Lightly oil and line the base of a 23cm loose-bottomed or springform cake tin with baking parchment.

To make the base, beat together the butter, icing sugar and salt until smooth. Add the egg, and beat well to combine. Add the flour and sifted cocoa powder, and bring together to form a dough. Wrap in clingfilm and chill in the fridge for 20 minutes.

Roll the rested dough on a lightly floured surface to about 3mm thick, then place the base of the cake tin on top and cut around it to give you a 23cm round dough base. Place in the bottom of the tin, lightly pressing into the edges. Chill for a further 20 minutes.

Heat the oven to 190°C/170°C fan/gas 5. Bake the chocolate base for 25 minutes until cooked and firm. Remove from the oven and leave to cool.

To make the filling, put the white chocolate on a baking tray lined with baking parchment or a silicone sheet. Put in the oven for 20 minutes until dark brown, almost burnt looking, stirring every 5 minutes. The chocolate will crumble but that is fine.

Meanwhile, soak the gelatine in a bowl of cold water to soften.

Put the milk, 100ml of the whipping cream and the vanilla seeds into a saucepan and bring to the boil.

Whisk together the egg yolks and sugar, then pour over the hot milk mixture. Pour back into the pan and cook over a low heat, stirring continuously until it thickly coats the back of a wooden spoon. Remove from the heat. Squeeze the excess water from the gelatine and stir into the pan until dissolved.

FOR THE CHOCOLATE GLAZE
65ml double cream
50g dark chocolate (minimum 70% cocoa solids), chopped into small pieces
35g caster sugar
15g cocoa powder, sifted

Transfer the caramelised chocolate to a mixing bowl and pour the hot vanilla custard mixture over the top. Cover and set aside for 10 minutes.

Blend the caramelised white chocolate mix with a stick blender until smooth and pass through a sieve. Leave to cool but do not chill.

Whisk the remaining 300ml whipping cream until it is holding its shape, and fold into the caramelised white chocolate mix. Pour on top of the chocolate base and level the surface with a palette knife. Freeze for a minimum of 3 hours.

While the mousse is setting, the chocolate glaze can be made. Heat 50ml of the double cream in a small saucepan, add the chocolate and briefly stir until it melts, creating a ganache.

Put the remaining tablespoon of double cream in a small saucepan with 50ml of water, caster sugar and cocoa powder. Bring to the boil. Strain through a sieve over the ganache and mix well.

Pour the ganache over the top of the chilled mousse and chill in the fridge for a further 1 hour.

When you are ready to serve, dip a palette knife into hot water and run it around the inside of the tin to release the sides of the cake. Carefully remove from the tin.

Cut into pieces with a hot sharp knife and serve straight away.

Salted caramel and chocolate tart with praline crunch

This certainly isn't the quickest of recipes, but the time and effort it needs are certainly well spent as it tastes amazing. Just do each stage at your own pace.

Praline paste is available from specialist cookshops and online, but if you can't get it you could substitute a nut butter such as almond or hazelnut.

Serves: 8–10
Preparation time: 1 hour 45 minutes,
    plus about 2 hours 30 minutes chilling
    time
Cooking time: 50 minutes

FOR THE PASTRY
60g soft butter
40g icing sugar, sifted
1 egg yolk and 1 egg, beaten
100g plain flour, plus extra for dusting
2 tsp cocoa powder
½ tsp baking powder
½ tsp ground cinnamon
15g ground hazelnuts

FOR THE PRALINE
40g caster sugar
20g unsalted butter
½ tsp sea salt
40g roasted hazelnuts

FOR THE SALTED CARAMEL
225g caster sugar
185ml whipping cream
40g butter
½ tsp sea salt
1 egg and 1 egg yolk
1½ tsp plain flour

To make the pastry, beat together the butter and sugar until lightly creamed. Add the egg yolk and beat well to combine. Sift in the flour, cocoa, baking powder and cinnamon and add the ground hazelnuts. Mix to form a thick, soft pastry. Wrap in clingfilm and chill in the fridge for at least 1 hour.

Roll the pastry on a lightly floured surface and use to line the base of a 20cm loose-bottomed cake tin. Press into the edges, but not up the sides of the tin. Chill in the fridge for 20 minutes.

Heat the oven to 180°C/160°C fan/gas 4. Line the pastry base with parchment and baking beans. Bake for 20 minutes and remove the baking beans and parchment. Continue to cook for a further 10 minutes until the pastry case is becoming firm. Brush with the beaten egg and cook for a further 2 minutes.

For the crunchy praline, put the sugar in a small heavy-based saucepan or frying pan. Place over medium heat and leave the sugar to melt and caramelise to a deep golden colour, swirling the pan occasionally to get even caramelisation. Add the butter and whisk in, then stir in the salt and nuts, coat well and transfer to parchment paper to cool. Once cold, crush with a rolling pin, or briefly whizz in a food processor and set aside.

To make the salted caramel, caramelise the sugar in a saucepan or frying pan, as above, but in a slightly larger pan this time. Remove from the heat and add the cream, then the butter to give you a smooth caramel sauce. Stir in the salt and leave to cool.

Once cool, mix the egg yolk with the flour, using a small whisk to remove any lumps. Add the whole egg. Mix into the cooled caramel sauce and pour into the cooked pastry case. Cook for 15–18 minutes until set. Leave to cool, then chill in the fridge.

To make the mousse, melt the chocolate over a pan of gently simmering water. Add the praline and lightly whip the double

FOR THE MOUSSE

250g milk chocolate, broken into small
  pieces
200ml double cream
40ml whipping cream
100g praline paste

and whipping cream together, then fold into the chocolate
praline mixture.

Spoon three-quarters of the mousse on top of the salted
caramel layer smooth over with a hot palette knife and chill
for about 40 minutes to set.

Run a palette knife around the outside of the tart and carefully
remove from the tin. Use the remaining quarter of the chocolate
praline mixture and spread all around the side of the tart.

Finish off by scattering over the crunchy praline and serve cut
into wedges.

Gin and tonic cheesecake

Surprisingly light and refreshing for a cheesecake, this is a must if you have G&T fans coming for dinner.

Makes: 8
Preparation time: 50 minutes plus
  4 hours setting
Cooking time: 20 minutes

groundnut or vegetable oil, for greasing

FOR THE BASE
75g soft butter
100g demerara sugar
180g plain flour
50g ground almonds

FOR THE FILLING
5 leaves gelatine
100g elderflower cordial
100g caster sugar
375g mascarpone cheese
160g cream cheese
150g crème fraîche
120ml gin
grated zest and juice of 3 lemons

FOR THE TOPPING
3 leaves gelatine
20g Stock Syrup (page 277)
120ml tonic
50ml gin

Preheat the oven to 200°C/180°C fan/gas 6. Lightly oil the inside of 8 ring moulds, 7.5cm diameter, and sit on a baking tray lined with parchment. Alternatively you can use 1 large loose-bottomed or spring-clip cake tin, approximately 23cm diameter, with the base lined with parchment.

To make the base, beat together the butter and sugar. Mix in the flour and almonds and press into the base of the ring moulds or cake tin. Bake in the oven for 15–20 minutes until golden. Leave to cool.

To make the filling, soak the gelatine in cold water for 5 minutes. Heat the elderflower cordial and caster sugar in a small pan until hot. Squeeze the excess water from the gelatine and stir into the elderflower until dissolved.

Put the remaining filling ingredients into a food processor, leaving a little of the lemon zest to one side, and blend until smooth. Add the elderflower cordial and gelatine mix and blend once more to combine.

Pour on top of the crumble bases and level the surface with a palette knife. Put in the fridge to set for at least 3 hours.

To make the tonic jelly topping, soak the gelatine in cold water for 5 minutes. Put the Stock Syrup and 20ml of water in a small pan and heat up. Squeeze the excess water from the gelatine and stir the gelatine into the pan until dissolved. Stir in the tonic and gin, and leave to cool. Once cool, carefully pour over the surface of the cheesecakes and chill, completely flat in the fridge, for at least 2 hours to set.

When you are ready to serve, dip a palette knife into hot water and run it around the inside of the rings or tin to release the cheesecake and carefully remove from the tin onto plates. Sprinkle the remaining lemon zest over and serve.

Buttermilk panna cotta with rhubarb and thyme crumble

A prepare-ahead dessert is always useful when entertaining, to give you more time to concentrate on other courses. Using buttermilk in a panna cotta makes it very light and refreshing to eat, so this recipe is ideal after a rich main course.

The thyme crumble will make plenty, so store the excess in an airtight container and use to scatter over other desserts such as ice cream or poached fruit.

Serves: 6
Preparation time: 30 minutes, plus at
    least 3 hours setting
Cooking time: 20 minutes

4 gelatine leaves (7 × 11cm strips)
200ml whole milk
400ml buttermilk
100g honey
groundnut or vegetable oil, for greasing
thyme leaves, to decorate

FOR THE RHUBARB
4 rhubarb sticks (use Yorkshire forced,
    when in season)
200g caster sugar
½ tsp rose water

FOR THE CRUMBLE
50g soft butter
50g demerara sugar
75g plain flour
25g ground almonds
1½ tsp thyme leaves

For the panna cotta, put the gelatine in a shallow bowl and cover with cold water. Leave to soften for 5 minutes.

Heat the milk in a small saucepan until hot but not boiling. Squeeze the water from the gelatine and stir the gelatine into the hot milk to completely dissolve. Mix in the buttermilk and honey. Strain into a jug.

Very lightly grease a 20cm pudding basin with a little oil. Pour the panna cotta mix in and pop in the fridge for 3 hours, or overnight, to set.

Cut the rhubarb into 3cm pieces, cutting them in half lengthways if they are particularly thick. Put the caster sugar in a saucepan along with 200ml of water and the rose water. Bring to the boil over high heat, reduce to a simmer and add the rhubarb. Cook gently for 5 minutes. Remove the rhubarb with a slotted spoon and chill in the fridge.

Place the pan back over the heat and cook the rhubarb juice for about 10–15 minutes, until it has reduced by about half and is the consistency of syrup. Remove from the heat and leave to cool completely before putting in the fridge to chill.

To make the crumble, preheat the oven to 200°C/180°C fan/gas 6 and line a baking sheet with baking parchment. Beat together the butter and sugar until creamy. Mix in the flour, almonds and thyme. Scatter the crumble mix onto the prepared baking sheet and bake for 15 minutes, shaking the tray halfway through to ensure an even colour, until golden and crunchy. Remove from the oven and allow to cool.

Remove the panna cotta from the fridge half an hour before serving. To serve, place 2 scoops onto each plate. Top with the poached rhubarb, pour over some syrup and finish with a scattering of crumble and some picked thyme.

Passion fruit jelly, lemon crème and lychee vodka sorbet

This is a fabulous end to a meal, with an amazing combination of flavours and textures that make your tastebuds feel so refreshed. For the restaurant we are able to source many different fruit liqueurs that are great for using in desserts. However, for cooking at home the passion fruit liqueur can be replaced by more readily available Cointreau, and lychee liqueurs can be swapped for a rose liqueur, or even lemon-flavoured vodka if you have trouble sourcing those.

Serves: 6
Preparation time: 30 minutes, plus
    3–4 hours freezing

FOR THE SORBET
2 × 400g tins lychees in juice, drained
250ml sparkling mineral water
80ml Stock Syrup (page 277)
40ml vodka
10ml lychee liqueur (optional)

FOR THE JELLY
2½ gelatine leaves
150ml Stock Syrup (page 277)
200g passion fruit purée or coulis
20ml Passoã (passion fruit) liqueur
    (optional)

FOR THE LEMON CRÈME
60g crème fraiche
60ml double cream
90g lemon curd

To make the sorbet, put the lychees in a blender and blitz until you have a smooth purée. Mix with the remaining sorbet ingredients and pass through a sieve. Churn in an ice cream machine until frozen, or if you don't have a machine follow the freezing method for Forest Fruit Sorbet on page 76.

For the jelly, soak the gelatine in a bowl of cold water for 5 minutes. Heat the stock syrup until just below boiling. Squeeze any excess water from the gelatine and stir the gelatine into the stock syrup until completely dissolved.

Mix in the passion fruit purée and, if using, the liqueur. Pass through a sieve into a jug.

Pour the jelly into individual glasses, to about a third full. Leave to set in the fridge for at least 2 hours.

For the lemon crème, whisk the crème fraîche and cream together until thickened, then fold in the lemon curd. Spoon or pipe on top of the set jelly so the glass is two-thirds full. Finish with a scoop of the lychee vodka sorbet.

Lemon curd filo crisp desserts with Earl Grey cream

This is a pretty complex dessert that has various exceptionally tasty elements. They're all made in advance, then assembled when serving, creating a fantastic end to your meal. I must stress, though, that every part of this recipe is completely doable at home, so don't be put off by the long list of ingredients and method. Just take one stage at a time and it will all come together.

The mini meringues used here are around 1cm in diameter. You can buy pre-made mini meringues, but if you find they are hard to come by, use larger ones broken into pieces, or of course you could make some yourself (see page 277).

You will have some leftover lemon curd mix after you've cut it into individual circles; this is great for filling pastry tart cases that you can make with the leftover filo pastry or for serving with the Yuzu and Maple Parfait (see page 221).

The lemon jam makes plenty and is great on toast or in other desserts, as it lasts ages in the fridge. You might even want to double up on the jam recipe, as I find it handy to have some in the fridge for emergency dessert making, such as stirring it into some whipped cream with chopped strawberries and serving with shortbread biscuits.

Serves: 6
Preparation time: 1 hour 15 minutes, plus 2 hours setting
Cooking time: 55 minutes

80g mini Meringues, or homemade Meringues, broken into pieces (page 277)

FOR THE LEMON CURD
grated zest of 3 lemons
175ml lemon juice (approx. 6 lemons)
275g caster sugar
2 gelatine leaves
3 whole eggs
2 egg yolks
185g cold butter, diced

To make the lemon curd, put the lemon zest, juice and sugar in a saucepan over medium heat. Stir until the sugar has dissolved, then bring to the boil.

Soak the gelatine in a bowl of cold water for 5 minutes.

Whisk together the whole eggs and egg yolks, and pour over the hot sweet juice, whisking as you pour. Return to the saucepan and stir over low heat until the mixture starts to thicken to the consistency of custard. Immediately remove from the heat before it overcooks and curdles. Squeeze the excess water from the gelatine and stir into the pan until dissolved.

Pour the curd into a food processor. Blitzing all the time, add the diced butter gradually. Once all the butter has been incorporated and the lemon curd is smooth, pass through a sieve to remove the zest. Pour into a deep baking tray, approximately 20 × 30cm, lined with clingfilm. You want the lemon curd to be around 2cm in thickness. Cool slightly, then put in the fridge for 2 hours to set firm.

FOR THE LEMON JAM
2 lemons
25g caster sugar

FOR THE FILO CRISPS
2–3 sheets filo pastry
30g butter, melted
caster sugar, for dusting

FOR THE EARL GREY CREAM
125ml double cream
5g Earl Grey tea leaves

To make the lemon jam, preheat the oven to 220°C/200°C fan/gas 6. Cut the lemons in half and remove any seeds. Place on a baking tray lined with baking parchment and bake for 35–45 minutes until they are dark golden.

Put the baked lemons into a blender or food processor and add the sugar and 25ml of water. Blend until you have a thick purée, removing any small seeds if you come across any. Set aside to cool completely.

While the oven is still on, make the filo crisps. Cut 12 circles of pastry using a 10cm pastry cutter. Place on a parchment-lined baking sheet and brush both sides lightly with melted butter. Lay another piece of parchment on top and place a baking sheet on top of the parchment, so the filo pastry is sandwiched inside.

Bake for 10 minutes until the pastry is golden and crisp. Remove from the oven and dust with sugar. Leave to cool.

To make the Earl Grey cream, heat half of the cream in a small saucepan until almost boiling and add the tea leaves. Cover with clingfilm and leave to infuse for 10 minutes. Strain into a bowl and chill in the fridge until cold. Add the remaining cream and whisk until thickened.

To assemble the desserts, remove the lemon curd from the fridge and, using an 8–9cm pastry cutter, cut out 6 circles. Place each one on a filo pastry crisp and sit on plates. Add a few mini meringues (or Meringues, broken into pieces), some dollops of Earl Grey cream and spoons of baked lemon jam. Top with another filo crisp and serve straight away.

BAKING

Rosemary oil bread

I like to make these at home for the family. We all love the smell of the rosemary as it's baking within the bread and find it hard to wait until they cool. These are ideal to serve with my Pumpkin Soup (see page 17).

Makes: 6 small loaves
Preparation time: 2 hours, plus
  24 hours infusing
Cooking time: 15 minutes

500g strong white bread flour
7g sachet fast-action or easy-bake yeast
1 tsp sugar
vegetable oil, for greasing

FOR THE ROSEMARY SALT
20g very finely chopped rosemary
50g flaked sea salt

FOR THE ROSEMARY OIL
100ml extra virgin olive oil
2 large sprigs of rosemary

To make the rosemary salt, mix together the rosemary and salt. Store in an airtight container and leave to infuse for at least 24 hours before using.

To make the rosemary oil, gently heat the oil in a saucepan. Add the rosemary. Cover and leave to infuse for at least 1 hour before using.

Mix together the flour, 10g of the rosemary salt, the yeast, sugar and 300ml of warm water to form a soft, smooth dough that leaves the sides of the bowl. This can be done by hand or using a standmixer fitted with a dough hook.

Cover the bowl with lightly oiled clingfilm and leave somewhere warm for about 1 hour, or until the dough has doubled in size.

Tip out onto a floured worktop and shape into a rectangle. Cut into 6 rectangles and place on two oiled baking trays. Cover with clingfilm and place somewhere warm to prove for 30 minutes.

Preheat the oven to 200°C/180°C fan/gas 4.

Bake the breads for 15 minutes, until lightly golden, brushing with the rosemary oil every now and then. Halfway through cooking, sprinkle the breads with the rosemary salt.

Enjoy warm.

Oatmeal soda bread

As far as breads go this has to be one of my favourites. Serve warm, cut into big chunks with plenty of Irish salted butter.

Makes: 20cm loaf
Preparation time: 10 minutes
Cooking time: 1 hour 5 minutes

vegetable oil, for greasing
100g medium rolled oats, plus
  2 tbsp extra
25g butter, plus extra for greasing
100ml natural yoghurt
200ml cold milk
25g soft light brown sugar
250g wholemeal flour
1½ tsp bicarbonate of soda
½ tsp sea salt

Preheat the oven to 200°C/180°C fan/gas 6. Grease and line a 20cm square cake tin with parchment.

Put the oats and 225ml of water in a large saucepan. Bring to a simmer and cook until you have a loose porridge consistency.

Remove from the heat and beat in the butter, followed by the yoghurt, milk and sugar. Stir in the flour, bicarbonate of soda and salt.

Pour into the prepared tin, level the surface and sprinkle over 2 tablespoons of extra oats. Cover with a layer each of baking parchment and foil.

Bake for 20 minutes, then remove the top layer of parchment and foil and bake for a further 45 minutes until deep golden and a skewer comes out clean when inserted into the centre.

Allow to cool for about 10 minutes in the tin before removing to cool further on a wire rack.

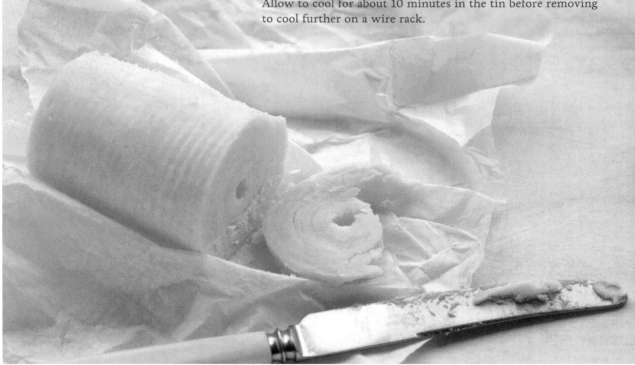

Malt loaf

I grew up eating malt loaf, and every time I make this it brings back many fond childhood memories. This chewy, sticky, fruity loaf with plenty of malt flavour won't disappoint — though do allow 1 week for the loaves to mature before eating for the best flavour. Try it as an accompaniment to cheese, too.

Makes: 2 loaves
Preparation time: 20 minutes, plus
    1 week maturing
Cooking time: 35–40 minutes

225ml brewed black tea using
    1 tea bag
250g malt extract, plus 2 tbsp extra,
    for glazing
125g dark muscovado sugar
450g dark raisins
butter, for greasing
3 eggs, lightly beaten
375g plain flour
1½ tsp baking powder
1 tsp bicarbonate of soda

Place the tea, 250g malt extract, sugar and raisins in a saucepan and gently heat until the sugar has dissolved. Cool slightly.

Preheat the oven to 180°C/160°C fan/gas 4. Grease and line two large loaf tins with baking parchment.

In a bowl, mix together the eggs, flour, baking powder and bicarbonate of soda. Add the cooled tea mixture and stir to combine.

Divide the mixture between the prepared tins and bake in the oven for 35–40 minutes, until a skewer comes out clean when inserted into the centre.

Remove and allow to cool for 10 minutes in the tin before turning out onto a wire rack.

To make the glaze, combine the 2 tablespoons of malt extract with 2 teaspoons of warm water to loosen. Brush over the tops of the loaves while they are still warm, then leave to cool completely.

Wrap each loaf in a layer of baking parchment and foil. Store for 1 week at room temperature to mature, then in the fridge for 2 weeks.

Walnut and raisin bread

I like to use both golden raisins (from the green grape) and dark raisins (from the red grape) for a contrast in colour and a slight difference in sweetness in this bread. Plus, to make sure it doesn't lack walnut flavour, I use walnut oil as well as chopped walnuts. It's ideal to serve with cheese, especially blue or mature cheeses, or with a rich terrine or pâté.

Makes: 2 loaves
Preparation time: up to 2½ hours
Cooking time: 20 minutes

500g strong bread flour, plus extra for
    dusting
2 tsp sea salt
18g fast-acting dried yeast
1 tbsp black treacle
3 tbsp walnut oil
vegetable oil, for greasing
75g golden raisins
75g dark raisins
150g walnut pieces

Put the flour and salt into a large mixing bowl and crumble in the yeast. Mix the treacle and oil in a bowl with 325ml of warm water and pour this into the flour. Mix and knead together to form a smooth, soft dough.

Cover the dough with lightly oiled clingfilm and put in a warm place for about 1 hour to prove until it has doubled in size.

Flour two baking sheets and set aside. Turn the dough onto a floured surface and lightly knead in the raisins and walnuts. Shape into two loaves and place on the floured baking sheets. Cover and allow to prove for a further 30 minutes–1 hour.

Preheat the oven to 220°C/220°C fan/gas 6. Dust the loaves with flour and bake for 15–20 minutes, or until golden and the loaves sound hollow when tapped. Transfer to a wire rack to cool.

Cornbread

This is a firm favourite at home with my children. I think it must be the sweetness that cornbread offers and the chunky pieces of sweetcorn running through. Try it as an accompaniment to chilli, or with scrambled eggs on the weekend.

Serves: 8–10
Preparation time: 15 minutes
Cooking time: 30–35 minutes

vegetable oil, for greasing
juice of ½ lemon
480ml milk
275g plain flour
225g polenta
1 tsp sea salt
20g baking powder
60g caster sugar
50g light brown sugar
2 eggs, beaten
110g butter, melted
250g tinned sweetcorn, drained, or frozen sweetcorn, defrosted and drained

Preheat the oven to 190°C/170°C fan/gas 5. Grease and line a 20 × 30cm loaf tin with baking parchment.

Stir the lemon juice into the milk and leave to sit for 5 minutes.

Put the flour, polenta, salt, baking powder, caster and brown sugars, eggs and butter in a large bowl and add the soured milk. Mix together until just combined, then fold in the sweetcorn.

Transfer to the prepared tin and level the surface with a palette knife.

Bake for 30–35 minutes, until the cornbread is just firm to the touch and lightly golden and a skewer comes out clean when inserted into the centre.

Remove and allow to cool completely before turning out from the tin and cutting into slices.

Wild garlic and rye bread

This is packed with flavour from the fragrant wild garlic and slightly sour rye flour. It may sound complex but it is nice and easy to prepare, and well worth a go. It's delicious served as an accompaniment to hard cheeses. Wild garlic is readily available in spring. As an alternative out of season, sage works well.

Makes: 1 loaf
Preparation time: 20 minutes, plus approx. 1 hour rising
Cooking time: 20 minutes

200g rye flour, plus extra for dusting
100g strong wholemeal bread flour
50g wheatgerm
2½ tsp fast-action dried yeast
1 tsp sea salt
3 tbsp golden syrup
50ml olive oil, plus extra for brushing
40g wild garlic leaves, chopped

Put both the flours, the wheatgerm, yeast and salt into the bowl of a standmixer fitted with a dough hook. Slowly mix together to combine.

In a bowl, mix the golden syrup, olive oil and 250ml of warm water. Slowly pour this mixture into the flours, with the mixer running, until everything comes together. Increase the speed slightly and mix for a further 5 minutes until you have an elastic dough.

Transfer the dough to a large oiled bowl and cover with a piece of oiled clingfilm. Leave to prove in a warm place for around 45 minutes until the dough rises by about a third of its size.

Turn the dough out onto a lightly floured surface and knead in the chopped garlic. Form into a round shape and sit on a lightly dusted baking sheet. Cover loosely with clingfilm and leave in a warm place for 15 minutes.

Preheat the oven to 200°C/180°C fan/gas 6.

Bake for 20–30 minutes, until the loaf is golden and sounds hollow when tapped underneath. Remove from the oven and leave to cool slightly before slicing.

Pistachio and apricot bread

This bread is enriched with milk and honey, which provides a soft, smooth dough and soft crust. The juicy sweetness from the apricots and the nutty crunch from the pistachios make this loaf the ideal partner for serving with cheese, especially strong blue cheeses such as Stilton or gorgonzola. That said, it's pretty hard to resist when still warm from the oven, cut into thick slices and spread with salted butter.

Makes: 1 loaf
Preparation time: 30 minutes, plus at least 1½ hours for rising
Cooking time: 35–40 minutes

500g strong white bread flour, plus extra for dusting
10g sea salt
7g fast-action dried yeast
300ml warm milk
100g honey
50g olive oil
100g pistachio nuts, toasted and chopped
100g dried apricots, diced
milk, for brushing
demerara sugar, for sprinkling

Place the flour, salt, yeast, milk, honey and oil in a mixing bowl. Bring together and knead well for about 10 minutes.

Knead in the pistachios and apricots, then transfer to a clean, lightly oiled bowl. Loosely cover with clingfilm and leave in a warm place to double in size.

Knock back the dough and shape into a loaf. Place on a floured baking tray. Brush with milk and dust lightly with the demerara sugar. Loosely cover with clingfilm and leave in a warm place to rise until it has doubled in size.

Preheat the oven to 180°C/160°C fan/gas 4.

Bake the loaf for 35–40 minutes until golden and it sounds hollow when tapped underneath.

Lift from the tray and leave to cool on a wire rack.

Gluten- and dairy-free bread

This recipe was originally created to serve in the restaurant, as we had many requests for breads that were gluten- or dairy-free. Making a bread that covered both bases was the ideal solution. I really love the flavour – it certainly hasn't been compromised at all when it comes to making this tasty loaf.

Makes: 1 loaf
Preparation time: 20 minutes, plus
   1 hour 10 minutes resting
Cooking time: 40–50 minutes

2 tsp fast-action dried yeast
140g dairy-free coconut milk yoghurt
35g golden linseeds
170g cornflour
100g gluten-free flour
35g polenta
7g xanthan gum
5g sea salt
5g caster sugar
35ml olive oil, plus extra for brushing

Grease and line a 20 × 30cm loaf tin with baking parchment.

Mix together the yeast and 275ml of warm water until the yeast has dissolved, then stir in the yoghurt and linseeds.

In a separate, larger bowl, mix together the cornflour, gluten-free flour, polenta, xanthan gum, salt and sugar. Pour in the yeast mixture and olive oil, then mix well to make a smooth, thin batter.

Leave for 5–10 minutes for the liquid to form into a sticky dough as the linseeds, cornflour and xanthan gum absorb the liquid and become gel-like in consistency.

Once the mixture is firm enough, knead on the work surface for around 15 seconds. Return to the bowl, cover with a piece of oiled clingfilm and leave to prove in a warm place for 30 minutes, until is has risen by about a third.

Transfer to the prepared tin and brush with olive oil. Cover with a piece of oiled clingfilm and leave in a warm place for a further 30 minutes.

Preheat the oven to 200°C/180°C fan/gas 6.

Bake for 40–50 minutes, until the loaf is golden and sounds hollow when tapped underneath.

Frangipane Christmas mince pies

These are my slightly indulgent twist on classic mince pies. They are exceptionally tasty and slightly simpler to make, with no pastry lid.

Makes: approx. 20
Preparation time: 50 minutes, plus minimum overnight marinating and chilling
Cooking time: 15 minutes

FOR THE FRUIT MINCE
50g dried and ready-to-eat prunes, finely chopped
25g dried cranberries, finely chopped
25ml brandy
½ cooking apple, grated
grated zest of ½ orange
½ nutmeg, grated
1½ tsp ground cinnamon
pinch of ground cloves
1 tsp black treacle
250g good-quality shop-bought mincemeat

FOR THE PASTRY
100g soft butter
145g caster sugar
225g strong white flour
1 tsp baking powder
pinch of sea salt
100ml double cream

FOR THE FRANGIPANE
50g soft butter
50g caster sugar
1 egg
50g ground almonds
25g plain flour
1 tbsp Amaretto or almond essence, plus extra for sprinkling

To prepare the fruit mince, soak the prunes and cranberries in brandy for 10 minutes. Mix in all the remaining ingredients and leave to marinate for as long as possible, but at least overnight.

Once marinated, take half the mince and blitz in a food processor to a paste. Combine the paste with the chunky mixture.

To make the pastry, mix the butter and sugar until just combined. Sift together the flour, baking powder and salt and add half to the butter and sugar. Mix to a smooth paste.

Add the remaining flour mixture and combine until the texture of breadcrumbs. Gradually add the cream and mix to form a smooth dough – you may not use all of the cream. Knead lightly until the dough becomes a smooth ball. Wrap in clingfilm and chill in the fridge for 2 hours.

Roll the pastry in between two sheets of baking parchment to about 3mm thick. Return to the fridge for 20 minutes.

To make the frangipane, beat together the butter and sugar until creamy. Add the egg, ground almonds, flour and Amaretto or almond essence. Spoon into a piping bag fitted with a plain nozzle.

Preheat the oven to 200°C/180°C fan/gas 6.

Use an 8cm round cutter to cut the pastry into circles and line 20 holes of two 12-cup muffin tins.

Stir the mince mixture well and use it to fill the pastry cases about two-thirds full. Pipe a good dollop of the frangipane mixture on top and bake in the oven for 15 minutes, until the frangipane is golden.

If you wish, douse with a good sprinkling of extra Amaretto when the pies come out of the oven, then leave to cool.

Rich chocolate cake (gluten-free)

I like to use soft brown sugar in this recipe, as it gives a mild toffee flavour and softer texture to this moreish cake. It is lovely served simply in slices, or you could just as easily transform it into a dessert with the addition of ice cream and a heavy dusting of cocoa powder combined with some ground cinnamon.

Serves: 8
Preparation time: 15 minutes
Cooking time: 40 minutes

175g soft butter, plus extra for greasing
175g light brown sugar
seeds from 1 vanilla pod
6 eggs, separated
175g dark chocolate, 70% cocoa solids,
  broken into pieces
175g ground almonds
½ tsp sea salt
cocoa powder, for dusting

Heat the oven to 180°C/160°C fan/gas 4. Grease and line the base of a 23cm loose-bottomed cake tin.

Beat together the butter, sugar and vanilla with an electric hand whisk until light and creamy.

Gradually add the egg yolks, beating well after each one is added.

Melt the chocolate in a bowl set over a pan of simmering water. Mix the melted chocolate, ground almonds and salt into the butter and sugar.

In a separate bowl, whisk the egg whites until they form soft peaks. Add a third to the chocolate mixture and combine, to loosen it. Then gently fold in the remaining egg whites using a large metal spoon.

Transfer to the prepared tin and bake for 40 minutes, until the cake is just firm in the centre and a skewer comes out clean when inserted into the middle. Remove from the oven. Cool slightly and dust with cocoa powder before serving.

Olive oil and rosemary cake with blackberry jam

Making a cake with olive oil gives such a lovely moist texture, and you can't taste the oil at all due to the lemon and rosemary running through. Served with this quick-cook blackberry jam, it makes a great afternoon tea treat. Alternatively, you could serve this as a dessert with Orange and Rosemary Custard (see page 279).

Serves: 8–10
Preparation time: 25 minutes
Cooking time: 40 minutes

4 eggs
200g caster sugar, plus 2 tbsp, to serve
grated zest and juice of 1 lemon, plus zest of ½ lemon, to serve
2 tsp finely chopped rosemary leaves
100ml olive oil
100g butter, melted, plus extra for greasing
200g ground almonds
50g polenta or semolina
50g plain flour
1 tsp baking powder

FOR THE JAM
250g fresh or frozen blackberries
2 tbsp blackberry liqueur or crème de cassis
50g caster sugar
5g pectin

Preheat the oven to 180°C/160°C fan/gas 4. Grease and line the base of a 23cm springform cake tin.

Put the eggs, caster sugar, lemon zest and rosemary in the bowl of a standmixer or mixing bowl and whisk until thick and creamy. The mixture should be at the ribbon stage – when the whisk is lifted from the mixture it should leave ribbons on the surface.

Slowly whisk in the lemon juice, oil and melted butter until combined.

In a bowl, mix together the almonds, polenta, flour and baking powder. Gently fold into the cake mixture.

Pour into the prepared tin and bake for 40 minutes, or until golden and just firm (cover after 30 minutes if the top is browning too quickly). When a skewer is inserted into the centre it should come out a little damp but not coated in cake mix. Remove from the oven and leave to cool.

To make the jam, put 150g of the blackberries in a small saucepan with the liqueur and 25g of the caster sugar. Bring to the boil. Sprinkle over the pectin, stir to dissolve and simmer for a further 5 minutes. Remove from the heat and leave to cool slightly. Stir in the remaining blackberries when just warm.

Carefully remove the cake from the tin, sprinkle with the sugar and lemon zest, and cut into wedges to serve with the jam.

Walnut burnt butter cakes

The beurre noisette (brown butter) used here really enhances the walnut flavour and gives a lovely deep golden colour to these light cakes. Once made they probably won't last long, as they taste so good, but if they are not eaten on the day of making, store in a cool place and warm to serve.

Makes: 12
Preparation time: 45 minutes
Cooking time: 15 minutes

125g walnut halves
25g plain flour
180g caster sugar
4 egg whites
125g unsalted butter
walnut oil, for greasing

Put the walnuts and flour in a food processor and blitz until finely ground. Add the caster sugar and egg whites and blend together to combine.

Melt the butter in a small saucepan over high heat. Reduce the heat to medium and cook until it becomes a golden, nutty brown colour. Slowly pour this into the walnut mixture, blending as you pour.

Transfer the mixture to a bowl and chill in the fridge for 30 minutes.

Preheat the oven to 200°C/180°C fan/gas 6. Lightly grease a 12-hole non-stick muffin tin with oil. Divide the cake mixture between the holes and bake for 15 minutes until lightly golden and just firm to the touch.

Remove from the tin and allow to cool completely on a wire rack.

Lime drizzle cake

I grew up with the classic lemon drizzle cake and thoroughly loved it, but now I prefer the aromatic tartness coming from the limes in this version. Fresh kaffir lime leaves can be found in Asian supermarkets, but frozen ones are fine to use in the recipe, too. This is one of those cakes that can be served anytime, to anyone. It's pretty impossible to say no!

Makes: 2 small or 1 large loaf
Preparation time: 15 minutes
Cooking time: 30–45 minutes

175g caster sugar
175g soft unsalted butter, plus extra
    for greasing
grated zest and juice of 4 limes
4 tbsp milk
2 eggs
175g self-raising flour
3 tbsp granulated sugar
2–3 kaffir lime leaves, finely sliced

Preheat the oven to 180°C/160°C fan/gas 4. Grease and line a 900g loaf tin or two 450g tins.

Place the caster sugar, butter and most of the lime zest in a bowl and beat together until pale and creamy. Add the milk, and then beat in the eggs, one at a time, adding a spoonful of flour with each egg to prevent the mixture from curdling. Mix in the remaining flour. Transfer to the prepared tin/tins and level the surface using a palette knife.

Bake in the oven for about 45 minutes for a large cake, or 30 minutes for the smaller ones, or until golden and a skewer comes out clean when inserted into the centre. Don't worry if the cake peaks in the middle and splits; it all adds character and will also give you a crunchier drizzle topping.

While the cake is cooking, bring the lime juice to the boil in a small saucepan and allow to reduce in quantity to about 3 tablespoons. Remove from the heat, leave to cool, then stir in the granulated sugar to dissolve. Add the remaining lime zest and the lime leaves and combine.

As soon as the cake comes out of the oven, prick several times with a skewer, and then slowly pour the lime syrup all over the top, letting it soak into the cake. Leave to cool completely in the tin before turning out and cutting into slices to serve.

Ginger cake with banana cream and salted caramel sauce

A thick spoonful of caramelised banana cream and warm salted caramel sauce poured over the top takes this simple ginger cake to another level. Use slightly over-ripe bananas as they have a far more intense flavour than under-ripe ones.

Serves: 6–8
Preparation time: 30 minutes
Cooking time: 30 minutes

45g stem ginger, in syrup
75g unsalted butter, plus extra
   for greasing
100g soft dark brown sugar
100g golden syrup
50ml milk
1 egg, lightly beaten
150g self-raising flour

FOR THE BANANA CREAM
50g caster sugar
1 banana, peeled and mashed
1 tbsp crème de banane (banana liqueur)
   (optional)
125ml double cream

FOR THE SALTED CARAMEL SAUCE
125g caster sugar
125ml double cream
20g unsalted butter
½ tsp sea salt

To make the cake, pound the ginger to a paste using a pestle and mortar (or alternatively, chop very finely). Set aside.

Preheat the oven to 200°C/180°C fan/gas 6. Grease and line a small loaf tin with baking parchment.

Put the butter, brown sugar and golden syrup in a bowl set over a pan of simmering water. Allow to melt together, stirring occasionally. Mix in the ginger, milk and egg. Add the flour and mix until just combined.

Pour into the prepared tin and bake for 25–30 minutes, until a skewer comes out clean when inserted into the centre. Cool on a wire rack.

For the banana cream, put the caster sugar in a small saucepan and add 2 tablespoons of water. Place over high heat and cook for 6–8 minutes, or until the sugar has caramelised to a rich golden colour. Add the mashed banana and stir until it has softened. Use a fork to mash to a smooth purée. Stir in the crème de banane, if using, and leave to cool.

Whisk the cream until it forms soft peaks. Stir in the banana purée until the cream thickens to firm peaks. Chill until needed.

To make the caramel sauce, put the caster sugar in a small saucepan and add 3 tablespoons of water. Place over high heat and cook for 6–8 minutes, until the sugar has caramelised to a rich golden brown. In a separate pan, heat the cream until it just comes to the boil. Add to the caramel along with the butter and salt, and whisk until combined.

Serve the cake cut into thick pieces with a spoonful of banana cream and the salted caramel poured over the top.

Lemon yoghurt cake (gluten- and dairy-free)

This dense citrusy cake was initially created for those who have to follow gluten- and dairy-free diets. That said, I highly recommend that everyone try it – it's quick to prepare and tastes amazing. I'll often serve this as a dessert with some fresh seasonal berries on the side.

Makes: 20cm cake
Preparation time: 15 minutes
Cooking time: 30 minutes

6 tbsp coconut oil, plus extra for
  greasing
130g dairy-free coconut yoghurt
5 eggs
grated zest and juice of 1 lemon
140g ground almonds
70g cornflour
130g soft light brown sugar
1 tsp baking powder
1 tsp bicarbonate of soda

FOR THE LEMON SYRUP
50g caster sugar
grated zest and juice of 1 lemon

Preheat the oven to 200°C/180°C fan/gas 6. Grease and line the base of a 20cm cake tin with baking parchment.

Put the coconut oil and yoghurt, eggs, lemon zest and juice in a food processor and blend until smooth. Add the almonds, cornflour, brown sugar, baking powder and bicarbonate of soda, then blend until combined.

Pour the mixture into the prepared tin and smooth over the top.

Bake for 30 minutes, until golden and just firm to the touch.

Make the syrup about 10 minutes before the cake is done. Place the caster sugar, lemon zest and juice in a small saucepan and bring to the boil. Simmer for 5 minutes.

Remove the cake from the oven and slowly pour over the syrup, covering the whole surface and allowing it to soak in before carefully removing the cake from the tin.

Carrot cake with cream cheese frosting

You really can't go wrong with a classic carrot cake. I like to make this in a round tin at home and cut it into wedges, though it can just as easily be made in a rectangular tin, then cut into small pieces and served as petits fours.

Makes: 20cm cake
Preparation time: 40 minutes
Cooking time: 1 hour

4 eggs
200ml vegetable oil, plus extra
    for greasing
300g caster sugar
350g carrots, grated
275g plain flour
100g walnuts, chopped
2 tsp bicarbonate of soda
1½ tsp baking powder
1½ tsp ground cinnamon
½ tsp ground allspice
seeds from 1 vanilla pod

FOR THE FROSTING
50g soft butter
50g icing sugar
280g cream cheese
grated zest of 1 lemon
80ml whipping cream

Preheat the oven to 200°C/180°C fan/gas 6. Lightly grease a 20cm round cake tin and line the base with baking parchment.

In a bowl, beat together the eggs and vegetable oil. Mix with the remaining cake ingredients until combined. Spoon into the prepared tin and level the surface with a palette knife.

Bake for 1 hour, until risen and just firm to the touch. Insert a skewer into the centre of the cake and if it comes out clean, it's cooked. (It may take a little longer depending on the moistness of the carrots.)

Allow to cool in the tin for 10 minutes before turning out onto a wire rack to cool completely.

To make the frosting, beat together the butter and icing sugar until light and fluffy.

In a separate bowl, beat the cream cheese and lemon zest until smooth. Gradually beat in the creamed butter and sugar mixture. Add the cream and beat again until combined.

Spread the frosting over the top of the cooled cake.

Peanut flapjacks

When you tuck into these it is quite hard to believe they are made from so few basic ingredients. The balance of sweet and salty with the peanuts is spot on. I think you might find you'll have to lock these away once made so they don't get eaten up in one go.

Makes: 12–16 pieces
Preparation time: 20 minutes
Cooking time: 30 minutes

150g blanched unsalted peanuts
300g rolled oats
½ tsp sea salt
225g butter, plus extra for greasing
300g muscovado sugar
30g golden syrup

Preheat the oven to 180°C/160°C fan/gas 5. Grease and line a 20 × 30cm tin with baking parchment.

Put the peanuts on a baking sheet and roast in the oven for 12–15 minutes, until golden. Cool slightly, then roughly chop. Tip into a large mixing bowl and add the oats and salt.

Put the butter, sugar and golden syrup in a saucepan and gently heat until the butter has melted and the sugar has dissolved. Pour over the oats and mix well.

Spoon into the prepared tin and bake for 30 minutes, until golden. When cooked, leave to cool in the tin. Once cool enough to handle but still slightly warm, cut into rectangles. Once cooled completely, store in an airtight container.

Custard cream biscuits

My homemade version of custard creams isn't as complicated as you might think, but you will need a sugar thermometer for the filling. I like to serve these with coffee after a meal. No matter how full people are, they will always find room for one or two of these! They are also perfect with a pot of tea in the afternoon.

Makes: about 30
Preparation time: 45 minutes
Cooking time: 20–25 minutes

275g plain flour, plus extra for dusting
50g custard powder
50g icing sugar, sifted
1 tsp baking powder
½ tsp sea salt
½ nutmeg, freshly grated
125g cold butter, diced
1 egg, lightly beaten
1 tbsp milk

FOR THE FILLING
125g caster sugar
2 egg yolks
seeds from 1 vanilla pod
150g very soft butter

FOR THE NUTMEG SUGAR
3 tbsp caster sugar
½ nutmeg, freshly grated

To make the filling, put the sugar and 4 tablespoons of water in a small saucepan. Place over high heat and occasionally swirl the pan around until the sugar reaches 120°C on a sugar thermometer. Try to avoid stirring the sugar while it cooks.

Put the egg yolks and vanilla seeds in a heatproof mixing bowl and whisk until light and fluffy. Gradually pour in the sugar syrup, whisking as you pour, and continue to whisk until the mixture is thick and cooled.

Add the very soft butter a little at a time and whisk until combined. Transfer to a piping bag with a plain nozzle and chill in the fridge until needed.

To make the biscuits, put all of the dry ingredients in a bowl and rub in the butter until you have a sand-like crumb texture. Make a well in the centre and add the beaten egg and milk and gradually incorporate until you have a soft dough.

Transfer the biscuit dough to a large piece of clingfilm or baking parchment and put another piece on top. Roll out to about 3mm thick. Place in the fridge to rest for 30 minutes.

Preheat the oven to 180°C/160°C fan/gas 4. In a bowl, mix together the caster sugar and nutmeg.

Cut the biscuit dough into rounds using a 4cm pastry cutter. Lightly dust the biscuits with the nutmeg sugar and bake for 15–18 minutes, until lightly golden and crisp.

Remove and allow to cool on a wire rack. When cooled, pipe the filling onto one half of the biscuits and sandwich them together with the remaining half.

Chocolate chunk cookies

Rich, chocolatey and irresistible – exactly as chocolate cookies should be. These are so good, it's worth doubling up on the dough and sticking half in the freezer, rolled into individual balls and ready to cook another time. Once baked, store in a container for up to 1 week (if they last that long).

Makes: approx. 20
Preparation time: 15 minutes
Cooking time: 12–15 minutes

125g soft butter
175g dark brown sugar
50g caster sugar
1 egg
175g plain flour
25g cocoa powder
1 tsp bicarbonate of soda
100g dark chocolate (70% cocoa solids),
   cut into chunks

Preheat the oven to 180°C/160°C fan/gas 4. Line two baking sheets with baking parchment or silicone mats.

Using an electric whisk or a standmixer, beat together the butter and both the sugars until light and creamy.

Beat in the egg and sift in the flour, cocoa powder and bicarbonate of soda. Stir to combine, then mix in the chocolate chunks.

Roll into golf-ball-size pieces and place on the prepared baking sheets, leaving space around each one to allow for spreading.

Bake for 12–15 minutes, until lightly golden. Leave to cool slightly on the tray for 5 minutes before transferring to a wire rack to cool completely. Store in an airtight container.

BASICS AND ACCOMPANIMENTS

Chicken stock

Makes: approx. 2 litres
Preparation time: 10 minutes
Cooking time: 2–3 hours

2 raw chicken carcasses, each cut
    into 4 pieces
2 onions, chopped
2 leeks, white part only, chopped
2 stalks celery, chopped
¼ bunch of thyme
2 bay leaves
½ tsp white peppercorns

Put the chicken carcasses in a large stock pot and cover with 4 litres of water. Bring to the boil and, once boiling, skim the surface to remove any discoloured foam/scum.

Reduce the heat until you have a simmer and then add the remaining ingredients. Leave to simmer for 2–3 hours over low heat, adding more water if the liquid reduces by more than two-thirds. Skim off any discoloured foam throughout cooking.

Strain the stock through a colander and then through a sieve.

Use the stock straight away or keep in the fridge for 3–4 days, removing any surface fat. Alternatively, freeze and use within 4 months.

Beef stock

Makes: approx. 1.5 litres
Preparation time: 10 minutes
Cooking time: 4½–6½ hours

3kg beef bones
3 tbsp vegetable oil
3 carrots, halved
4 onions, quartered
½ bulb garlic
3 celery sticks, halved
½ bunch of thyme
1 bay leaf
3 tbsp tomato purée

Heat the oven to 220°C/200°C fan/gas 7. Put the beef bones into a couple of roasting trays and roast for about 30 minutes until dark golden, turning every so often.

Meanwhile, heat the oil in a large stock pot. Add the carrots, onions, garlic and celery. Cook over high heat until dark golden.

Stir in the thyme, bay leaf and tomato purée. Cook for a few minutes.

Lift the roasted bones from the tray and drain off the excess fat. Add the bones to the stock pot. Add 4 litres of cold water and bring to the boil. Skim any discoloured foam/scum from the surface and reduce the heat to low. Simmer for 4–6 hours, skimming occasionally.

Strain the stock through a colander and then through a sieve into a clean pan. Bring to the boil and reduce to approximately 1.5 litres.

Use straight away or cool and chill in the fridge, using within 3–4 days. Remove any surface fat before using. Alternatively, freeze and use within 4 months.

Vegetable stock

Makes: approx. 1.5 litres
Preparation time: 20 minutes, plus
  24 hours chilling
Cooking time: 10 minutes

2 leeks, chopped
6 carrots, chopped
3 onions, chopped
3 celery stalks, chopped
4 garlic cloves
1 star anise
1 tsp coriander seeds
½ tsp white peppercorns
2 bay leaves
¼ bunch of thyme

Put the leeks, carrots, onions, celery and garlic in a large stock pot and cover with 2 litres of cold water. Bring to the boil over high heat. Skim off any scum, reduce the heat to medium and cook for 8 minutes.

Lightly crush the star anise, coriander seeds and white peppercorns. As soon as the 8 minutes are up, add to the stock pot along with the fresh herbs and lemon. Simmer for a further 2 minutes, then remove from the heat. Leave until cool, then cover and transfer to the fridge for 24 hours.

Strain the vegetable stock through a fine sieve and discard the vegetables. Keep covered in the fridge and use within 3–4 days. Alternatively, freeze and use within 4 months.

Mayonnaise

Makes: 300ml
Preparation time: 5 minutes

2 egg yolks
1 tsp white wine vinegar
1 tsp English mustard
150ml olive oil
150ml vegetable oil
sea salt and freshly ground black pepper

Put the egg yolks, vinegar, mustard and a pinch of salt in a mixing bowl and mix together with a balloon whisk.

Slowly drizzle in the oil, whisking continuously until thick and emulsified. Taste, and add more seasoning, if you like, and keep in the fridge for up to 3 days.

Roast garlic aioli

Makes: approx. 250ml
Preparation time: 20 minutes
Cooking time: 45 minutes

2 garlic bulbs
175ml olive oil, plus extra to rub
3 egg yolks
1 tbsp white wine vinegar
½ tsp Dijon mustard
50ml vegetable oil
squeeze of lemon juice
sea salt

Preheat the oven to 180°C/160°C fan/gas 4.

Remove a quarter of the top of the garlic. Sit the garlic in a piece of foil and rub with a little olive oil and some salt. Wrap and roast in the oven for 45 minutes.

When cool enough to handle, squeeze out the soft-roasted garlic into a bowl. Mash with the back of a fork until completely smooth. Cover and set aside to cool completely.

Put the egg yolks in a bowl and, using a balloon whisk, mix in the vinegar and Dijon mustard. Put both oils in a jug and slowly drizzle into the egg yolk mixture, continuously whisking as you do so. When you have a thick mayonnaise consistency, stir in the garlic purée and season with salt and a squeeze of lemon juice to taste. If not using straight away, store in the fridge where it will keep for up to 3 days.

Ranch dressing

Makes: 350ml
Preparation time: 10 minutes

200ml crème fraîche
150g mayonnaise
1 tsp English mustard powder
½ tsp smoked paprika
1 tbsp chopped flat-leaf parsley
1 tbsp chopped coriander
1 tsp sweet chilli sauce
sea salt and freshly ground black pepper

Mix all of the ingredients together in a bowl. Season with salt and black pepper. Keep chilled in the fridge.

Basic vinaigrette

Makes: approx. 470ml
Preparation time: 5 minutes

360ml olive oil
40ml extra virgin olive oil
60ml white wine vinegar
10ml sherry vinegar
¼ tsp agave syrup
sea salt and freshly ground black pepper
1 bay leaf and a couple of sprigs of thyme
   and tarragon (optional)

Whisk together all of the ingredients and season to taste.

The dressing can be used straight away; however, if you add the bay leaf, thyme and tarragon sprigs to the vinaigrette, once made store it at room temperature for up to 1 week to allow the herb flavours to infuse into the dressing.

Chorizo jam

Makes: approximately 350g
Preparation time: 15 minutes
Cooking time: 40 minutes

2 tbsp vegetable oil
1 onion, chopped
2 garlic cloves, crushed
1 tsp ground allspice
1 tbsp sweet/mild smoked paprika
2 tbsp chopped fresh thyme
½ tsp sea salt
50ml balsamic vinegar
2 tbsp tomato purée
1 tbsp black treacle
200g cooking chorizo dulce, peeled
   and very finely chopped
100g smoked streaky bacon, very finely
   chopped

Heat the oil in a saucepan. Add the onion, garlic, allspice, paprika, thyme and salt, and cook for 5 minutes over medium heat, until the onion softens. Stir in the balsamic vinegar and cook for 5 minutes, until it becomes syrupy.

Add the tomato purée and treacle and cook for a further 3 minutes.

Add the chorizo and bacon, stirring frequently for 30 minutes over low heat.

Serve warm or store in sterilised jars and keep for up to 1 month in the fridge.

Bacon jam

Makes: approximately 300g
Preparation time: 15 minutes
Cooking time: 40 minutes

2 tbsp vegetable oil
250g smoked streaky bacon, very finely
   chopped
1 onion, chopped
1 garlic clove, crushed
4 coriander seeds, crushed
1 tsp smoked paprika
1 tbsp sherry vinegar
½ tsp black pepper
2 tbsp tomato purée
1 tbsp black treacle

Heat the oil in a pan over medium-high heat. Add the bacon, onion and garlic, and cook until the bacon is golden and the onions are soft.

Add all of the remaining ingredients and cook over low heat, stirring frequently, for 30 minutes.

Serve warm or store in sterilised jars and keep for up to 1 month in the fridge.

Onion marmalade

Makes: approx. 350ml
Preparation time: 10 minutes
Cooking time: 30 minutes

1 tbsp vegetable oil
3 onions, diced
3 garlic cloves, chopped
1 tsp ground cumin
150ml white wine vinegar
200g caster or granulated sugar
1 tsp black onion seeds (nigella seeds)
2 tsp mustard seeds
4 black peppercorns

Heat the oil in a saucepan and gently sauté the onions and garlic until softened but not coloured. Add the cumin and continue to sauté for 1 minute before adding the vinegar, 75ml of water, the sugar, onion seeds, mustard seeds and peppercorns. Cook over moderate heat until the liquid has evaporated.

Leave the onion mix to cool. When cold, the marmalade is ready to use.

Mango chutney

Makes: approx. 350ml
Preparation time: 10 minutes
Cooking time: 15 minutes

250ml mango purée
½ tbsp vegetable oil
1 small onion, diced
1½ garlic cloves, chopped
½ tsp ground cumin
75ml white wine vinegar
100g caster or granulated sugar
½ tsp nigella seeds
1 tsp mustard seeds
sea salt
2 black peppercorns

Put the mango purée in a wide saucepan and bring to a simmer over medium-low heat. Cook very slowly until it reduces in volume by about a third to give you approximately 150ml.

Meanwhile, heat the oil in a saucepan and gently sauté the onion and garlic until softened but not coloured. Add the cumin, and continue to sauté for 1 minute before adding the vinegar, sugar, nigella seeds, mustard seeds, salt, peppercorns and 75ml of water. Cook over medium heat for 5 minutes, until the liquid has evaporated.

Leave both the onion mix and mango purée to cool and chill separately. When cold, mix together and the mango chutney is ready to use. Keeps for 2 weeks.

Prawn butter

Makes: 250g
Preparation time: 20 minutes
Cooking time: 10 minutes

2 tbsp vegetable oil
shells from 500g raw prawns (available
   from fishmongers)
250g unsalted butter, diced
½ red chilli, deseeded and roughly chopped
½ bunch of tarragon

Heat the oil in a saucepan over high heat. When it starts to smoke, add the prawn shells and fry until they are golden.

Add the butter, chilli and tarragon. Allow the butter to melt, then simmer for 5 minutes over medium-low heat.

Strain the prawn butter through a fine sieve and leave to cool and set. Store in the fridge.

Salsa verde

Serves: 4
Preparation time: 5 minutes

2 heaped tbsp finely chopped tarragon leaves
2 heaped tbsp finely chopped parsley leaves
20g capers
zest and juice of 1 lemon
125ml extra virgin olive oil

Place all of the ingredients in a food processor and pulse until you have a chunky sauce.

Romesco sauce

Makes: approx. 200ml
Preparation time: 5 minutes
Cooking time: 5 minutes

100g roasted red peppers, deseeded and
   skin removed, or piquillo peppers,
   roughly chopped
50g flaked toasted almonds
3 tbsp olive oil
½ tsp smoked paprika
2 tbsp chopped flat-leaf parsley
2 tsp tomato purée
splash of dry sherry
sea salt and freshly ground black pepper

Place all of the ingredients in a food processor and pulse until you have a chunky paste. Season with salt and black pepper and serve.

Meringues

Makes: 6–8 large meringues
Preparation time: 10 minutes
Cooking time: 1½ hours

wedge of lemon
3 egg whites
200g caster sugar

Preheat the oven to 120°C/100°C fan/gas ½. Line two large baking sheets with non-stick baking parchment.

Rub the lemon wedge around the inside of an electric mixing bowl. Add the egg whites and whisk using a low-medium speed until you have soft peaks.

Increase the heat to high and gradually add the sugar, continuously whisking until you have a stiff meringue.

Spoon 6–8 dollops of the meringue mixture onto the baking parchment, spreading apart to allow for a slight increase in volume when cooking.

Bake in the oven for 1½ hours or until crisp and firm.

Leave to cool and use straight away or store in an airtight container for up to 1 week.

Stock syrup

Makes: approx. 250ml
Preparation time: 5 minutes

250g caster sugar

Put the caster sugar and 500ml of cold water in a saucepan and gently heat until the sugar dissolves. Bring to the boil and simmer for 2 minutes. Remove from the heat and leave to cool.

Store for 2 months in the fridge.

Vanilla custard

Serves: 6
Preparation time: 10 minutes
Cooking time: 5 minutes

300ml milk
300ml double cream
seeds from 1 vanilla pod
6 egg yolks
60g caster sugar

Put the milk, cream and vanilla seeds in a saucepan and bring to the boil.

Meanwhile, put the egg yolks and sugar in a medium-sized bowl and mix together.

Slowly whisk the hot vanilla milk into the egg yolks and pour back into the pan.

Cook over a gentle heat, stirring continuously, for about 5 minutes until the custard coats the back of a spoon. Take care not to boil the custard as the egg yolks will scramble. Strain and cool.

Burnt honey custard

Serves: 6
Preparation time: 10 minutes
Cooking time: 5 minutes

125g honey
300ml milk
300ml double cream
6 egg yolks
30g caster sugar

Put the honey in a saucepan and bring to the boil. Allow to caramelise until a deep golden colour. Cool slightly.

Meanwhile, warm the milk in a separate saucepan, then add to the honey. Put the pan over low heat and stir until the honey has dissolved. Add the cream and bring to the boil.

Mix the egg yolks with the caster sugar and strain the hot honey milk on top.

Cook over gentle heat, stirring continuously, for about 5 minutes until the custard coats the back of a spoon. Take care not to boil the custard as the egg yolks will scramble. Strain and cool.

Orange and rosemary custard

Serves: 6
Preparation time: 10 minutes
Cooking time: 5 minutes

300ml milk
300ml double cream
zest of 1 orange, grated
2 sprigs of rosemary
6 egg yolks
60g caster sugar

Bring the milk and cream to the boil as in the Vanilla Custard recipe opposite, swapping the vanilla seeds for the orange zest and rosemary. Leave to infuse for 10 minutes, then strain through a sieve on top of the egg yolks and caster sugar.

Cook over gentle heat, stirring continuously, for about 5 minutes until the custard coats the back of a spoon. Take care not to boil the custard as the egg yolks will scramble. Strain and cool.

Earl Grey custard

Serves: 6
Preparation time: 10 minutes
Cooking time: 5 minutes

300ml milk
300ml double cream
1½ tbsp Earl Grey tea leaves
6 egg yolks
60g caster sugar

Bring the milk and cream to the boil as in the Vanilla Custard recipe opposite, swapping the vanilla seeds for the tea leaves. Leave to infuse for 10 minutes, then strain through a sieve on top of the egg yolks and caster sugar.

Cook over gentle heat, stirring continuously, for about 5 minutes until the custard coats the back of a spoon. Take care not to boil the custard as the egg yolks will scramble. Strain and cool.

CONVERSION CHARTS

DRY WEIGHTS

METRIC	IMPERIAL	METRIC	IMPERIAL
5g	¼oz	500g	1lb 2oz
8/10g	⅓oz	550g	1lb 3oz
15g	½oz	600g	1lb 5oz
20g	¾oz	625g	1lb 6oz
25g	1oz	650g	1lb 7oz
30/35g	1¼oz	675g	1½lb
40g	1½oz	700g	1lb 9oz
50g	2oz	750g	1lb 10oz
60/70g	2½oz	800g	1¾lb
75/85/90g	3oz	850g	1lb 14oz
100g	3½oz	900g	2lb
110/120g	4oz	950g	2lb 2oz
125/130g	4½oz	1kg	2lb 3oz
135/140/150g	5oz	1.1kg	2lb 6oz
170/175g	6oz	1.25kg	2¾lb
200g	7oz	1.3/1.4kg	3lb
225g	8oz	1.5kg	3lb 5oz
250g	9oz	1.75/1.8kg	4lb
265g	9½oz	2kg	4lb 4oz
275g	10oz	2.25kg	5lb
300g	11oz	2.5kg	5½lb
325g	11½oz	3kg	6½lb
350g	12oz	3.5kg	7¾lb
375g	13oz	4kg	8¾lb
400g	14oz	4.5kg	9¾lb
425g	15oz	6.8kg	15lb
450g	1lb	9kg	20lb
475g	1lb 1oz		

568ml = 1 UK pint (20fl oz) | 16fl oz = 1 US pint

LIQUID MEASURES

METRIC	IMPERIAL	CUPS
15ml	½fl oz	1 tbsp (level)
20ml	¾fl oz	
25ml	1fl oz	⅛ cup
30ml	1¼fl oz	
50ml	2fl oz	¼ cup
60ml	2½fl oz	
75ml	3fl oz	
100ml	3½fl oz	⅜ cup
110/120ml	4fl oz	½ cup
125ml	4½fl oz	
150ml	5fl oz	⅔ cup
175ml	6fl oz	¾ cup
200/215ml	7fl oz	
225ml	8fl oz	1 cup
250ml	9fl oz	
275ml	9½fl oz	
300ml	½ pint	1¼ cups
350ml	12fl oz	1½ cups
375ml	13fl oz	
400ml	14fl oz	

METRIC	IMPERIAL	CUPS
425ml	15fl oz	
450ml	16fl oz	2 cups
500ml	18fl oz	2¼ cups
550ml	19fl oz	
600ml	1 pint	2½ cups
700ml	1¼ pints	
750ml	1⅓ pints	
800ml	1 pint 9fl oz	
850ml	1½ pints	
900ml	1 pint 12fl oz	3¾ cups
1 litre	1¾ pints	1 quart (4 cups)
1.2 litres	2 pints	1¼ quarts
1.25 litres	2¼ pints	
1.5 litres	2½ pints	3 US pints
1.75/1.8 litres	3 pints	
2 litres	3½ pints	2 quarts
2.2 litres	3¾ pints	
2.5 litres	4⅓ pints	
3 litres	5 pints	
3.5 litres	6 pints	

OVEN TEMPERATURES

°C	°F	GAS MARK	DESCRIPTION
110	225	¼	cool
130	250	½	cool
140	275	1	very low
150	300	2	very low
160/170	325	3	low to moderate
180	350	4	moderate
190	375	5	moderately hot
200	400	6	hot
220	425	7	hot
230	450	8	hot
240	475	9	very hot

INDEX